AF893914

The Ultimate Book of Baby Afghans

Bobbie Matela, Managing Editor
Carol Wilson Mansfield, Art Director
Mary Ann Frits, Editorial Director
Kathy Wesley, Pattern Editor
Kelly Robinson and Sandy Scoville, Editorial Staff
Graphic Solutions inc-chgo, Book Design

For a full-color catalog including books of knit and crochet designs, write to:

American School of Needlework®
Consumer Division
1455 Linda Vista Drive
San Marcos, CA 92069

Shown on front cover: Baa Baa Blankie; Baby's Garden.

Afghans designers: Rings of Love by Mike Cates; Baby's Garden and Little Angel by Mary Ann Frits; Rock-a-Bye Baby, Baby Peach Blossom, Buttercup for Baby, Beautiful Dreams, Blue Ribbon Baby, Lavender and Lace, Lullaby and Goodnight, and So Pretty by Ann Kirtley; Baa Baa Blankie and Kitty Cat Lullaby by Becky Stevens; Baby Seashells, Bright Crayons, Little Fisherman, and Pink Roses by Rita Weiss; Bundles of Joy, Rainbow Rounds, Rainbow Sprinkles, Rosebuds for Baby, and Sweetheart Mile-a-Minute by Kathy Wesley.

Patterns tested and models made by Mary Ann Frits, Tammy Hebert, Ann Kirtley, Lori Llewellyn, Melody Long, Georgia Nordman, Carly Poggemeyer, Dolores Roberts, Landee Roth, Mary Somerset, Hannelore Southard, Ruby Townsend, and Kathy Wesley.

We have made every effort to ensure the accuracy and completeness of these instructions. We cannot, however, be responsible for human error, typographical mistakes, or variations in individual work.

©1998 by American School of Needlework®, Inc.;
ASN Publishing, 1455 Linda Vista Drive, San Marcos, CA 92069

ISBN: 0-88195-844-1 All rights reserved. Printed in U.S.A. 3 4 5 6 7 8 9

Introduction

It would be wonderful if every baby could feel the warmth of a cozy afghan created by the loving fingers of a dear knitter or crocheter.

The Ultimate Book of Baby Afghans includes 22 exciting afghans—a collection you'll go to time and again when looking for an afghan for a new arrival.

There are designs for every baby occasion, from lacy afghans for formal christenings to engaging bright, colorful afghans for playtime in the park. Whether you're in the mood for making an exquisite fancy-stitch afghan or a quick mile-a-minute or ripple afghan, you'll always find a new interesting afghan that suits your fancy.

Afghan Directory

Abbreviations and Symbols

Knit Abbreviations

CB . . . . . cable back
CF . . . . . cable front
inc. . . . . . increase
K . . . . . knit
P . . . . . purl
K2 tog . . . . . knit 2 together
P2 tog . . . . . purl 2 together
PSSO . . . . . pass slipped stitch over
tbl . . . . . through back loop
yb . . . . . yarn in back
yf . . . . . yarn in front

Crochet Abbreviations

BL(s) . . . . . back loop(s)
ch(s) . . . . . chain(s)
CL(s) . . . . . cluster(s)
dc . . . . . double crochet(s)
dtrc . . . . . double triple crochet(s)
FL(s) . . . . . front loop(s)
hdc . . . . . half double crochet(s)
lp(s) . . . . . loop(s)
PC(s) . . . . . popcorn(s)
rnd(s) . . . . . round(s)
sc . . . . . single crochet(s)
trc . . . . . triple crochet(s)

Knit and Crochet Abbreviations

beg . . . . . begin(ning)
dec . . . . . decrease (-ing)
Fig. . . . . . figure
patt . . . . . pattern
prev . . . . . previous
rem . . . . . remain(ing)
rep . . . . . repeat(ing)
sk . . . . . skip
sl . . . . . slip
sl st(s) . . . . . slip stitch(es)
sp(s) . . . . . space(s)
st(s) . . . . . stitch(es)
tog . . . . . together
YO . . . . . yarn over

***** An asterisk (or ****** double asterisks) is used to mark the beginning of a portion of instructions to be worked more than once; thus, "rep from ***** twice more" means after working the instructions once, repeat the instructions following the asterisk twice more (3 times in all).

† The dagger (or †† double daggers) identifies a portion of instructions that will be repeated again later in the same row or round.

— The number after a long dash at the end of a row or round indicates the number of stitches you should have when the row or round has been completed. The long dash can also be used to indicate a completed stitch such as a decrease, a shell, or a cluster.

( ) Parentheses are used to enclose instructions which should be worked the exact number of times specified immediately following the parentheses, such as "(2 sc in next dc, sc in next dc) twice." They are also used to set off and clarify a group of stitches that are to be worked all into the same space or stitch, such as "(2 dc, ch 1, 2 dc) in corner sp."

[ ] Brackets and **( )** parentheses are used to provide additional information to clarify instructions.

Join - join with a sl st unless otherwise specified.

The patterns in this book are written using United States terminology. Terms which have different English equivalents are noted below.

United States	**English**
single crochet (sc)	double crochet (dc)
half double crochet (hdc)	half treble (htr)
double crochet (dc)	treble (tr)
triple crochet (trc)	double treble (dtr)
double triple crochet (dtrc)	triple treble (trtr)
skip (sk)	miss
slip stitch (sl st)	slip stitch (ss) or "single crochet"
gauge	tension
yarn over (YO)	yarn over hook (YOH)

Stitch Guide

Chain - ch:
YO, draw through lp on hook.

Single Crochet - sc:
Insert hook in st, YO and draw through, YO and draw through both lps on hook.

Half Double Crochet - hdc:
YO, insert hook in st, YO, draw through, YO and draw through all 3 lps on hook.

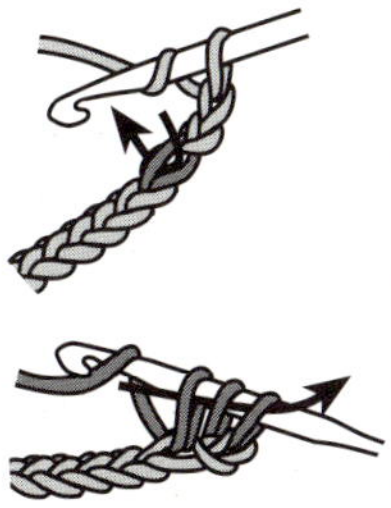

Double Crochet - dc:
YO, insert hook in st, YO, draw through, (YO and draw through 2 lps on hook) twice.

Triple Crochet - trc:
YO twice, insert hook in st, YO, draw through, (YO and draw through 2 lps on hook) 3 times.

Slip Stitch - sl st:
(a) **Used for Joinings**
Insert hook in indicated st, YO and draw through st and lp on hook.

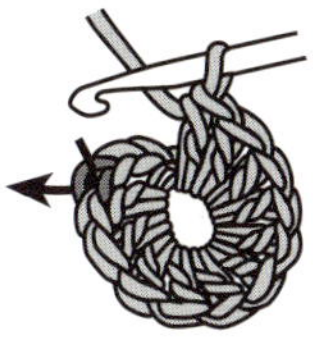

(b) **Used for Moving Yarn Over**
Insert hook in st, YO, draw through st and lp on hook.

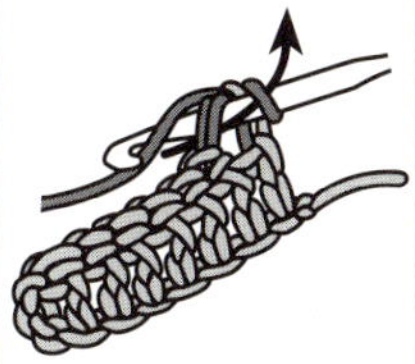

Front Loop - FL:
The front loop is the loop toward you at the top of the stitch.

Back Loop - BL:
The back loop is the loop away from you at the top of the stitch.

Post:
The post is the vertical part of the stitch.

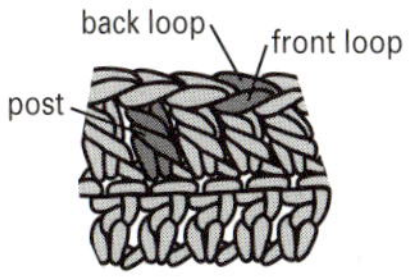

Overcast Stitch is worked loosely to join crochet pieces.

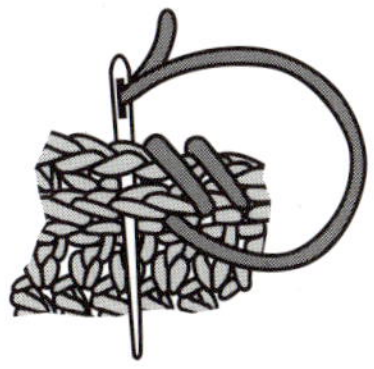

Metric Conversion Charts

INCHES INTO MILLIMETERS & CENTIMETERS (Rounded off slightly)

inches	mm	cm	inches	cm	inches	cm	inches	cm
1/8	3		5	12.5	21	53.5	38	96.5
1/4	6		5 1/2	14	22	56	39	99
3/8	10	1	6	15	23	58.5	40	101.5
1/2	13	1.3	7	18	24	61	41	104
5/8	15	1.5	8	20.5	25	63.5	42	106.5
3/4	20	2	9	23	26	66	43	109
7/8	22	2.2	10	25.5	27	68.5	44	112
1	25	2.5	11	28	28	71	45	114.5
1 1/4	32	3.2	12	30.5	29	73.5	46	117
1 1/2	38	3.8	13	33	30	76	47	119.5
1 3/4	45	4.5	14	35.5	31	79	48	122
2	50	5	15	38	32	81.5	49	124.5
2 1/2	65	6.5	16	40.5	33	84	50	127
3	75	7.5	17	43	34	86.5		
3 1/2	90	9	18	46	35	89		
4	100	10	19	48.5	36	91.5		
4 1/2	115	11.5	20	51	37	94		

mm - millimeter cm - centimeter

CROCHET HOOKS CONVERSION CHART

U.S.	1/B	2/C	3/D	4/E	5/F	6/G	8/H	9/I	10/J	10 1/2/K
English	12	11	10	9	8	7	6	5	4	2
Continental-mm	2.25	2.75	3.25	3.5	3.75	4.25	5	5.5	6	6.5

KNITTING NEEDLES CONVERSION CHART

U.S.	0	1		2		3	4	5		6	7	8	9	10	10 1/2			11	13	15
Metric(mm)	2	2 1/4	2 1/2	2 3/4	3	3 1/4	3 1/2	3 3/4	4		4 1/2	5	5 1/2	6	6 1/2	7	7 1/2	8	9	10
U.K.	14	13		12	11	10		9	8		7	6	5	4	3	2	1	0	00	000

Fringe

Basic Instructions

Cut a piece of cardboard half as long as specified in instructions for strands plus ½" for trimming allowance. Wind yarn loosely and evenly lengthwise around cardboard. When card is filled, cut yarn across one end. Do this several times, then begin fringing; you can wind additional strands as you need them.

Single Knot Fringe

Hold specified number of strands for one knot of fringe together, then fold in half. Hold afghan with right side facing you. Use crochet hook to draw folded end through space or stitch from right to wrong side **(Figs 1** and **2)**, pull loose ends through folded section **(Fig 3)** and draw knot up firmly **(Fig 4)**. Space knots as indicated in pattern instructions.

Fig 1

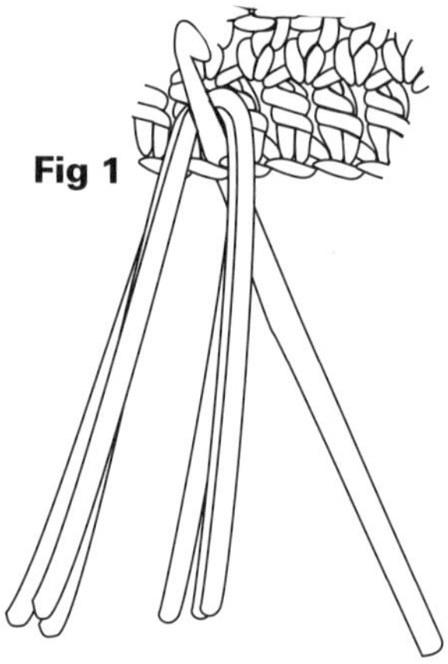

Fig 2

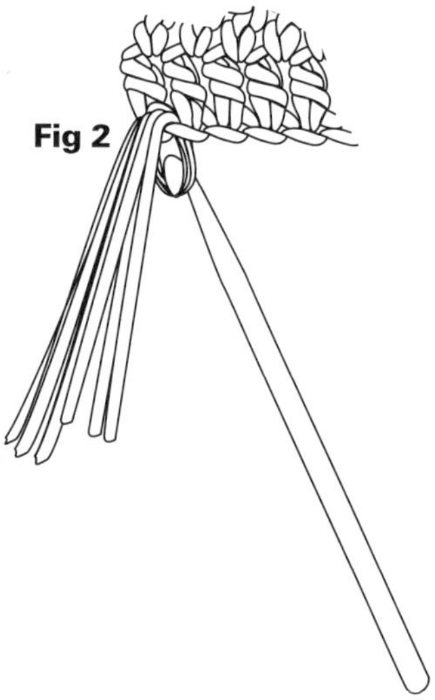

Fig 3

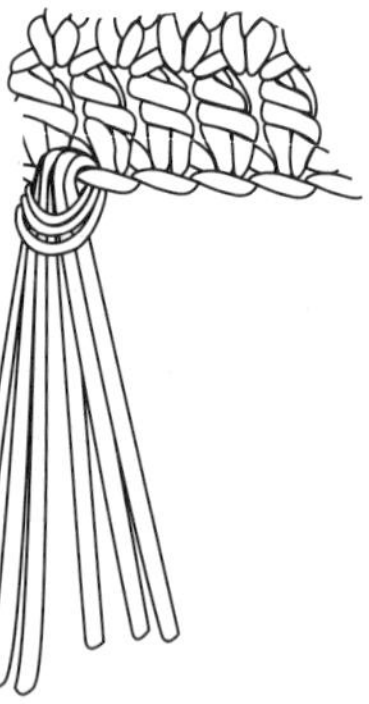

Fig 4

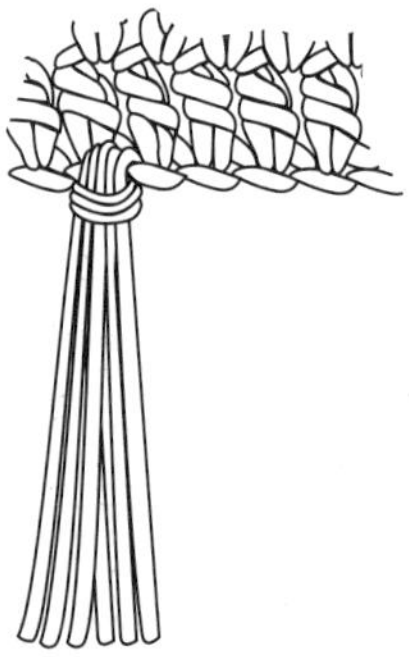

Double Knot Fringe

Begin by working Single Knot Fringe completely across one end of afghan. With right side facing you and working from left to right, take half the strands of one knot and half the strands in the knot next to it, and knot them together **(Fig 5)**.

Fig 5

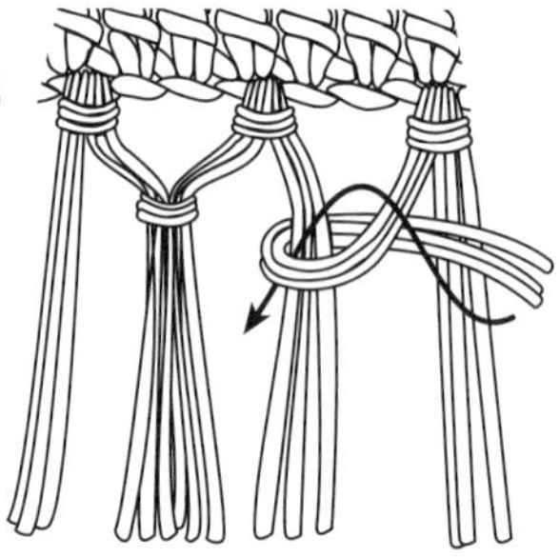

Triple Knot Fringe

First work Double Knot Fringe. Then working again on the right side from left to right, tie third row of knots as in **Fig 6**.

Fig 6

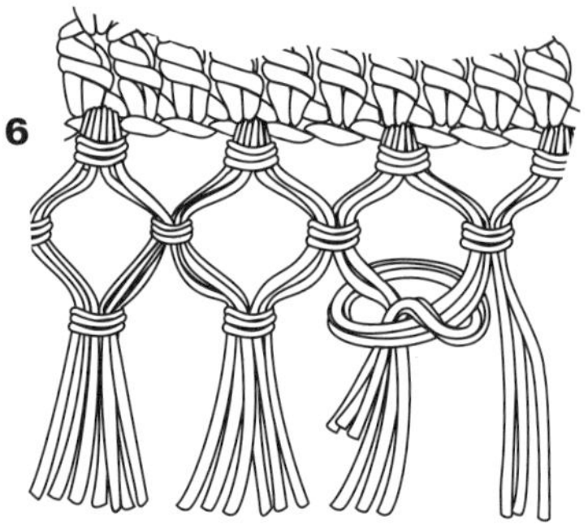

Baby Peach Blossom

Size:
About 35" x 39"

Materials:
Baby weight yarn, 11 oz (1870 yds, 330 g) peach
Size D aluminum crochet hook, or size required for gauge

Gauge:
6 dc = 1"

Pattern Stitches

Cluster (CL):
Keeping last lp of each trc on hook, 3 trc in sp indicated; YO and draw through all 4 lps on hook—CL made.

Double Crochet Cluster (dcCL):
Keeping last lp of each dc on hook, 3 dc in st indicated; YO and draw through all 4 lps on hook–dcCL made.

Instructions

Ch 183 loosely.

Center

Row 1 (right side):
Dc in 4th ch from hook (beg 3 skipped chs count as a dc) and in next 2 chs, ch 3, sk next 3 chs; * dc in next 7 chs, ch 3, sk next 3 chs; rep from * 16 times more; dc in next 4 chs. Ch 3 (counts as first dc on following rows), turn.

Row 2:
Dc in next 2 dc, ch 2, in next ch-3 sp work [CL (see Pattern Stitches), ch 2] twice; * sk next dc, dc in next 5 dc, ch 2, in next ch-3 sp work (CL, ch 2) twice; rep from * 16 times more; sk next dc, dc in next 2 dc and in 3rd ch of beg 3 skipped chs. Ch 3, turn.

Row 3:
Dc in next dc, ch 2, CL in next CL; ch 2, CL in next ch-2 sp; ch 2, CL in next CL; ch 2, sk next dc; * dc in next 3 dc, ch 2, CL in next CL; ch 2, CL in next ch-2 sp; ch 2, CL in next CL; ch 2, sk next dc; rep from * 16 times more; dc in next dc and in 3rd ch of turning ch-3. Ch 5 (counts as first dc and ch-2 sp on following rows), turn.

Row 4:
Dc in next CL, (2 dc in next ch-2 sp, dc in next CL) twice; * ch 3, sk next 3 dc, dc in next CL, (2 dc in next ch-2 sp, dc in next CL) twice; rep from * 16 times more; ch 2, sk next dc, dc in 3rd ch of turning ch-3. Ch 4 (counts as first dc and ch-1 sp on following row), turn.

Row 5:
CL in next ch-2 sp; ch 2, sk next dc, dc in next 5 dc, ch 2; * in next ch-3 sp work (CL, ch 2) twice; sk next dc, dc in next 5 dc, ch 2; rep from * 16 times more; CL in ch-2 sp formed by first 2 chs of turning ch-5; ch 1, dc in next ch. Ch 4 (counts as first trc on following row), turn.

Row 6:
Trc in next ch-1 sp, ch 2, CL in next CL; ch 2, sk next dc, dc in next 3 dc, ch 2, CL in next CL; ch 2; * CL in next ch-2 sp; ch 2, CL in next CL; ch 2, sk next dc, dc in next 3 dc, ch 2, CL in next CL; ch 2; rep from * 16 times more; trc in ch-1 sp formed by turning ch-4 and in next ch. Ch 3, turn.

Row 7:
2 dc in next ch-2 sp; dc in next CL, ch 3, sk next 3 dc, dc in next CL; * (2 dc in next ch-2 sp, dc in next CL) twice; ch 3, dc in next CL; rep from * 16 times more; 2 dc in next ch-2 sp; sk next trc, trc in 4th ch of turning ch-4. Ch 3, turn.

Rows 8 through 79:
Rep Rows 2 through 7 twelve times more.

Rows 80 through 84:
Rep Rows 2 through 6. At end of Row 84, do not ch 3; do not turn.

Finish off and weave in all ends.

Border

Hold center with right side facing you and Row 84 at top; with peach, make lp on hook and join with an sc in first trc in upper right-hand corner.

Rnd 1:
Working across Row 84, sc in same trc, 2 sc in next trc; sc in each CL, in each ch-2 sp, in each dc, and in each trc across to last trc and turning ch-4; 2 sc in last trc; 3 sc in 4th ch of turning ch-4; working along next side in sps formed by edge sts and turning chs, 4 sc in each of Rows 84 and 83; 3 sc in each of Rows 82 through 3; 4 sc in each of Rows 2 and 1; working across bottom in unused lps and unused chs of beg ch, 2 sc in each of first 2 lps; sc in each unused lp and ch to last 2 lps; 2 sc in next lp; 3 sc in next lp; working along next side in sps formed by edge sts and turning chs, 4 sc in each of Rows 1 and 2; 3 sc in each of Rows 3 through 82; 4 sc in each of Rows 83 and 84; join in joining sc—884 sc.

continued on page 9

Rnd 2:
Ch 1, sc in same sc and in next 13 sc; ch 4, sk next 3 sc; * sc in next 14 sc, ch 4, sk next 3 sc; rep from * around; join in first sc—52 ch-4 sps.

Rnd 3:
Sl st in next 3 sc, ch 1, sc in same sc as last sl st made and in next 2 sc; ch 3, sk next 2 sc, sc in next 3 sc, ch 1, sk next 3 sc, in next ch-4 sp work (dc, ch 1) 6 times; * sk next 3 sc, sc in next 3 sc, ch 3, sk next 2 sc, sc in next 3 sc, ch 1, sk next 3 sc, in next ch-4 sp work (dc, ch 1) 6 times; rep from * around; join in first sc.

Rnd 4:
Sl st in next 2 sc and in next ch-3 sp, ch 1, sc in same sp; ch 2, [dcCL (see Pattern Stitches on page 7) in next ch-1 sp, ch 2] 7 times; * sc in next ch-3 sp, ch 2, (dcCL in next ch-1 sp, ch 2) 7 times; rep from * around; join in first sc.

Rnd 5:
Ch 1, sc in same sc; ch 3, (dcCL in next dcCL, ch 3) 7 times; * sc in next sc, ch 3, (dcCL in next dcCL, ch 3) 7 times; rep from * around; join in first sc.

Rnd 6:
Rep Rnd 5.

Rnd 7:
Sl st in next 3 chs and in next dcCL, ch 1, sc in same dcCL; (5 dc in next ch-3 sp, sc in next dcCL) 6 times; * sk next ch-3 sp, next sc, and next ch-3 sp; sc in next dc, (5 dc in next ch-3 sp, sc in next dcCL) 6 times; rep from * around; join in first sc.

Finish off and weave in ends.

Baa Baa Blankie

Size:
About 38" x 44"

Materials:
Sport weight yarn, 25 oz (2375 yds, 750 g) ecru; 1/2 oz (48 yds, 15 g) black
Size G aluminum crochet hook, or size required for gauge
Size 16 tapestry needle

Gauge:
4 sc = 1"
5 sc rows = 1"

Pattern Stitch

Cluster (CL):
Keeping last lp of each dc on hook, 2 dc from front to back to front around post (see Stitch Guide on page 5) of st indicated; YO and draw through all 3 lps on hook—CL made.

Instructions

With ecru, ch 151 loosely.

Row 1 (wrong side):
Sc in 2nd ch from hook and in each rem ch—150 sc. Ch 1, turn.

Row 2 (right side):
Sc in each sc. Ch 1, turn.

Rows 3 through 15:
Rep Row 2.

Row 16:
Sc in first 19 sc; * † CL (see Pattern Stitch) around next sc on 2nd row below; on working row, sk next sc, sc in next sc, CL around next sc on 2nd row below; on working row, sk next sc, sc in next 3 sc, CL around next sc on 2nd row below; on working row, sk next sc, sc in next sc, CL around next sc on 2nd row below; on working row, sk next sc †; sc in next 17 sc; rep from * 3 times more, then rep from † to † once; sc in next 18 sc. Ch 1, turn.

Row 17:
Sc in each st. Ch 1, turn.

Row 18:
Sc in first 19 sc; * † CL around next CL; on working row, sk next sc, sc in next sc, CL around next CL; on working row, sk next sc, sc in next 3 sc, CL around next CL; on working row, sk next sc, sc in next sc, CL around next CL; on working row, sk next sc †; sc in next 17 sc; rep from * 3 times more, then rep from † to † once; sc in next 18 sc. Ch 1, turn.

Row 19:
Sc in first 17 sc; * (ch 4, sc in BL of next st) 10 times; sc through both lps of next 16 sc; rep from * 3 times more; (ch 4, sc in BL of next st) 10 times; sc through both lps of next 19 sc. Ch 1, turn.

Row 20:
Sc in first 19 sc; * † working in unused lps of Row 18, dc in next 10 lps †; sc in next 16 sc; rep from * 3 times more, then rep from † to † once; sc in next 17 sc. Ch 1, turn.

Row 21:
Sc in first 16 sc; * (ch 5, sc in BL of next st) 12 times; sc through both lps of next 14 sc; rep from * 3 times more; (ch 5, sc in BL of next st) 12 times; sc through both lps of next 18 sc. Ch 1, turn.

Row 22:
Sc in first 18 sc; * † working in unused lps of Row 20, dc in next 12 lps †; sc in next 14 sc; rep from * 3 times more, then rep from † to † once; sc in next 16 sc. Ch 1, turn.

Row 23:
Rep Row 21.

Row 24:
Sc in first 18 sc; * † working in unused lps of Row 22, dc in next 12 lps †; sc in next 14 sc; rep from * 3 times more, then rep from † to † once; sc in next 16 sc. Ch 1, turn.

Row 25:
Sc in first 17 sts; * (ch 5, sc in BL of next dc) 10 times; sc through both lps of next 16 sc; rep from * 3 times more; sc in next 19 sc. Ch 1, turn.

Row 26:
Sc in first 19 sc; * † working in unused lps of Row 24, dc in next 10 lps †; sc in next 16 sc; rep from * 3 times more, then rep from † to † once; sc in next 17 sc. Ch 1, turn.

Row 27:
Sc in first 18 sts; * † (ch 5, sc in BL of next dc) 8 times †; sc in next 18 sts; rep from * 3 times more, then rep from † to † once; sc in next 20 sc. Ch 1, turn.

continued on page 12

Row 28:
Sc in first 20 sc; * † working in unused lps of Row 26, dc in next 8 lps †; sc in next 18 sc; rep from * 3 times more, then rep from † to † once; sc in next 18 sc. Ch 1, turn.

Row 29:
Sc in first 18 sc; * (ch 5, sc in BL of next dc) 8 times; sc through both lps of next 18 sc; rep from * 3 times more; (ch 5, sc in BL of next dc) 8 times; sc through both lps of next 20 sc. Ch 1, turn.

Row 30:
Sc in first 20 sc; * † working in unused lps of Row 28, dc in next 8 lps †; sc in next 18 sts; rep from * 3 times more, then rep from † to † once; sc in next 18 sc. Ch 1, turn.

Row 31:
Sc in each st. Ch 1, turn.

Row 32:
Sc in each sc. Ch 1, turn.

Rows 33 through 43:
Rep Row 32.

Row 44:
Sc in first 32 sc; * † CL around next sc on 2nd row below; on working row, sk next sc, sc in next sc, CL around next sc on 2nd row below; on working row, sk next sc, sc in next 3 sc, CL around next sc on 2nd row below; on working row, sk next sc, sc in next sc, CL around next sc on 2nd row below; on working row, sk next sc †; sc in next 17 sc; rep from * twice more, then rep from † to † once; sc in next 31 sc. Ch 1, turn.

Row 45:
Sc in each st. Ch 1, turn.

Row 46:
Sc in first 32 sc; * † CL around next CL; on working row, sk next sc, sc in next sc, CL around next CL; on working row, sk next sc, sc in next 3 sc, CL around next CL; on working row, sk next sc, sc in next sc, CL around next CL; on working row, sk next sc †; sc in next 17 sc; rep from * twice more, then rep from † to † once; sc in next 31 sc. Ch 1, turn.

Row 47:
Sc in first 30 sc; * (ch 4, sc in BL of next st) 10 times; sc through both lps of next 16 sc; rep from * twice more; (ch 4, sc in BL of next st) 10 times; sc through both lps of next 32 sc. Ch 1, turn.

Row 48:
Sc in first 32 sc; * † working in unused lps of Row 46, dc in next 10 lps †; sc in next 16 sc; rep from * twice more, then rep from † to † once; sc in next 30 sc. Ch 1, turn.

Row 49:
Sc in first 29 sc; * (ch 5, sc in BL of next st) 12 times; sc through both lps of next 14 sc; rep from * twice more; (ch 5, sc in BL of next sc) 12 times; sc through both lps of next 31 sc. Ch 1, turn.

Row 50:
Sc in first 31 sc; * † working in unused lps of Row 48, dc in next 12 lps †; sc in next 14 sc; rep from * twice more, then rep from † to † once; sc in next 29 sc. Ch 1, turn.

Row 51:
Rep Row 49.

Row 52:
Sc in first 31 sc; * † working in unused lps of Row 50, dc in next 12 lps †; sc in next 14 sc; rep from * twice more, then rep from † to † once; sc in next 29 sc. Ch 1, turn.

Row 53:
Sc in first 30 sc; * † (ch 5, sc in BL of next dc) 10 times †; sc in next 16 sts; rep from * twice more, then rep from † to † once; sc in next 28 sc. Ch 1, turn.

Row 54:
Sc in first 32 sc; * † working in unused lps of Row 52, dc in next 10 lps †; sc in next 12 sc; rep from * twice more, then rep from † to † once; sc in next 30 sc. Ch 1, turn.

Row 55:
Sc in first 31 sts; * † (ch 5, sc in BL of next dc) 8 times †; sc in next 18 sts; rep from * twice more, then rep from † to † once; sc in next 28 sc. Ch 1, turn.

Row 56:
Sc in first 33 sc; * † working in unused lps of Row 54, dc in next 8 lps †; sc in next 13 sc; rep from * twice more, then rep from † to † once; sc in next 31 sc. Ch 1, turn.

Row 57:
Sc in first 31 sc; * (ch 5, sc in BL of next dc) 8 times; sc through both lps of next 18 sc; rep from * twice more; (ch 5, sc in BL of next dc) 8 times; sc through both lps of next 33 sc. Ch 1, turn.

Row 58:
Sc in first 33 sc; * † working in unused lps of Row 56, dc in next 8 lps †; sc in next 18 sc; rep from * twice more, then rep from † to † once; sc in next 31 sc. Ch 1, turn.

Rows 59 through 71:
Rep Rows 31 through 43.

Rows 72 through 183:
Rep Rows 16 through 71 twice.

Rows 184 through 199:
Rep Rows 16 through 31.

Row 200:
Sc in each sc. Ch 1, turn.

Rows 201 through 213:
Rep Row 200.

Edging

Rnd 1:
3 sc in first sc—corner made; sc in next 148 sc, 3 sc in next sc—corner made; working along next side in edge sc, sk Row 213, sc in Rows 212 through 2; working across bottom in unused lps of beg ch, 3 sc in first lp—corner made; sc in next 148 lps, 3 sc in next lp—corner made; working along next side in edge sc, sk Row 1, sc in Rows 2 through 212; join in FL of first sc—730 sc.

Note: Mark 2nd sc of each corner on Rnd 1.

Rnd 2:
Ch 1, sc in same lp; ch 5; working in FLs only, * sc in next sc, ch 5; rep from * around; join in first sc.

Rnd 3:
Working in unused lps of Rnd 1, sl st in first lp, ch 3 (counts as a dc), 3 dc in next lp (marked st)—corner made; * dc in each lp to next marked st, 3 dc in next lp—corner made; rep from * twice more; dc in each lp to beg ch-3; join in 3rd ch of beg ch-3.

Rnd 4:
Ch 1, sc in same ch as joining; ch 5; * sc in next dc, ch 5; rep from * around; join in first sc.

Finish off and weave in all ends.

Finishing

Referring to **Chart A** and **Fig 1** cross stitch lamb faces using tapestry needle and 2 strands of black.

Chart A

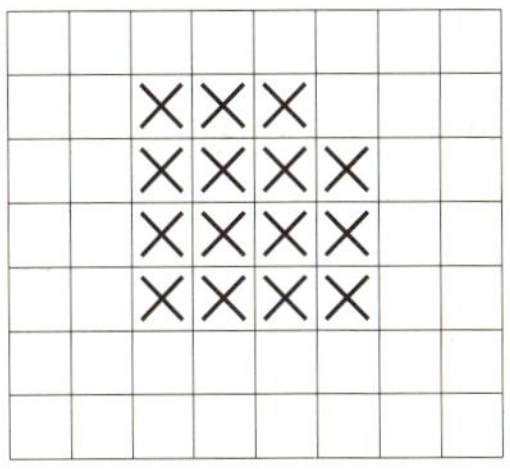

Key
X = black

Fig 1

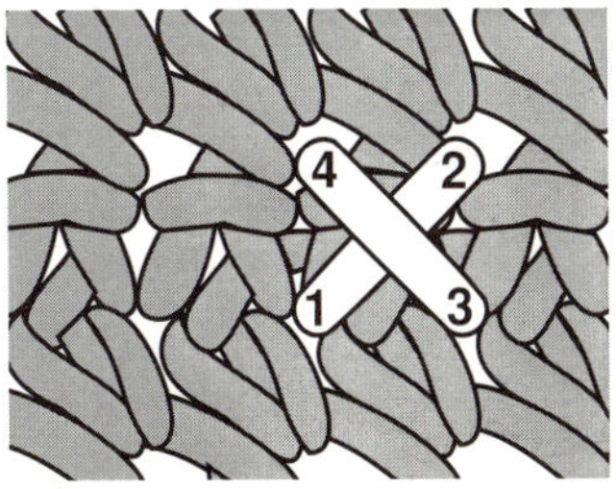

Bring needle up at 1, down at 2, up at 3, and down at 4 to complete the stitch.

Baby Seashells

Size:
About 34" x 44"

Materials:
Sport weight yarn, 16 oz (1520 yds, 480 g) yellow
Size 6, 36" circular knitting needle, or size required for gauge

Gauge:
5 sts = 1" in stockinette stitch (knit one row, purl one row)

Instructions

Cast on 188 sts.

Row 1:
Knit.

Rows 2 through 6:
Rep Row 1.

Row 7 (right side)**:**
K4; * K1, YO, (K1, P3) 4 times; K1, YO; rep from * 9 times more; K4—208 sts.

Row 8:
K4; * P1, (P1, K3) 4 times; P3; rep from * 9 times more; K4.

Row 9:
K4; * K2, YO, (K1, P3) 4 times; K1, YO, K1; rep from * 9 times more; K4—228 sts.

Row 10:
K4; * P2, (P1, K3) 4 times; P4; rep from * 9 times more; K4.

Row 11:
K4; * K3, YO, (K1, P3) 4 times; K1, YO, K2; rep from * 9 times more; K4—248 sts.

Row 12:
K4; * P3, (P1, K3) 4 times; P5; rep from * 9 times more; K4.

Row 13:
K4; * K4, YO, (K1, P2 tog, P1) 4 times; K1, YO, K3; rep from * 9 times more; K4—228 sts.

Row 14:
K4; * P4, (P1, K2) 4 times; P6; rep from * 9 times more; K4.

Row 15:
K4; * K5, YO, (K1, P2 tog) 4 times; K1, YO, K4; rep from * 9 times more; K4—208 sts.

Row 16:
K4; * P5, (P1, K1) 4 times; P7; rep from * 9 times more; K4.

Row 17:
K4; * K6, YO, (sl 1, K1, PSSO) 4 times; K1, YO, K5; rep from * 9 times more; K4—188 sts.

Row 18:
K4; purl to last 4 sts, K4.

Rows 19 through 320:
Rep Rows 7 through 18 twenty-six times more.

Rows 321 through 326:
Knit.

Bind off as to knit.

Baby's Garden

Size:
About 32" x 32"

Materials:
Baby weight yarn, 9 oz (1530 yds, 270 g) green; 2 oz (340 yds, 60 g) pink; 1 1/2 oz (255 yds, 45 g) white
Size D aluminum crochet hook, or size required for gauge
Size 16 tapestry needle

Gauge:
6 sc = 1"

Instructions

Square (make 29 squares with pink flower centers and 20 squares with white flower centers)

Flower Center:
Note: Flower Center is worked on wrong side.

Ch 4, join to form a ring.

Rnd 1 (wrong side)**:**
Ch 1, (sc in ring, ch 3) 4 times; join in first sc.

Rnd 2 (right side)**:**
Sl st in next ch-3 sp, ch 1, in same sp work (sc, 5 dc, sc)—petal made; in each rem ch-3 sp work (sc, 5 dc, sc)—petal made; working in front of first petal; join in base of first sc of prev rnd—4 petals.

Rnd 3:
Ch 1, sc in same sp; ch 3, working in front of petals, (sc in base of next sc on Rnd 1, ch 3) 3 times; join in first sc.

Rnd 4:
Sl st in next ch-3 sp, ch 1, in same sp work (sc, hdc, dc, 3 trc, dc, hdc, sc)—petal made; in each rem ch-3 sp work (sc, hdc, dc, 3 trc, dc, hdc, sc)—petal made; working in front of first petal; join in base of first sc—4 petals.

Rnd 5:
Ch 1, sc in same sp; ch 3, working in front of petals, sc in base of 2nd trc of same petal, ch 3; * sc in base of first sc on next petal, ch 3, sc in base of 2nd trc of same petal, ch 3; rep from * twice more; join in first sc.

Rnd 6:
Sl st in next ch-3 sp, ch 1, in same sp work (sc, hdc, dc, 3 trc, dc, hdc, sc)—petal made; in each rem ch-3 sp work (sc, hdc, dc, 3 trc, dc, hdc, sc)—petal made; join in first sc—8 petals. Finish off.

Leaf Base:
Hold center with right side facing you; working behind petals made in Rnd 6, join green in base of 2nd trc of any petal.

Rnd 1 (right side)**:**
Ch 1, sc in same sp; ch 3, (sc in base of 2nd trc of next petal, ch 3) 7 times; join in first sc.

Rnd 2:
Sl st in next ch-3 sp, ch 3 (counts as a dc), 8 dc in same sp; * † ch 2, sc in next ch-3 sp, ch 2 †; 9 dc in next ch-3 sp; rep from * twice more, then rep from † to † once; join in 3rd ch of beg ch-3.

Rnd 3:
Ch 2, dc in next 6 dc, dec over next 2 dc [to work dec: (YO, draw up lp in next dc, YO, draw through 2 lps on hook) twice; YO and draw through all 3 lps on hook—dec made]; * † ch 3, (sc in next ch-2 sp, ch 3) twice †; dec over next 2 dc; dc in next 5 dc, dec over next 2 dc; rep from * twice more, then rep from † to † once; join in first dc.

Rnd 4:
Ch 2, dc in next 4 dc, dec; * † ch 3, (sc in next ch-3 sp, ch 3) 3 times †; dec; dc in next 3 dc, dec; rep from * twice more, then rep from † to † once; join in first dc.

Rnd 5:
Ch 2, dc in next 2 dc, dec; * † ch 3, (sc in next ch-3 sp, ch 3) 4 times †; dec; dc in next dc, dec; rep from * twice more, then rep from † to † once; join in first dc.

Rnd 6:
Ch 2, (YO, draw up lp in next dc, YO, draw through 2 lps on hook) twice; YO and draw through all 3 lps on hook—beg cluster made; * † ch 3, (sc in next ch-3 sp, ch 3) 5 times †; (YO, draw up lp in next dc, YO, draw through 2 lps on hook) 3 times; YO and draw through all 4 lps on hook—cluster made; rep from * twice more, then rep from † to † once; join in beg cluster.

Rnd 7:
Ch 1, 3 sc in same cluster—corner made; * † 3 sc in each of next 6 ch-3 sps †; 3 sc in next cluster—corner made; rep from * twice more, then rep from † to † once; join in BL of first sc—84 sc.

continued on page 18

TRAV-LER

Rnd 8:
Ch 2 (counts as an hdc), working in BLs only, 3 hdc in next sc—hdc corner made; * hdc in next 20 sc; 3 hdc in next sc—hdc corner made; rep from * twice more; hdc in next 19 sc; join in 2nd ch of beg ch-2.

Finish off and weave in all ends.

Assembly

Referring to **Diagram A** for placement, join squares in following manner. Hold two squares with right sides together, carefully matching stitches. With tapestry needle and green and starting and ending in 2nd hdc of matching corners, sew with overcast st (see Stitch Guide on page 5) through BLs only. Join remaining squares in same manner.

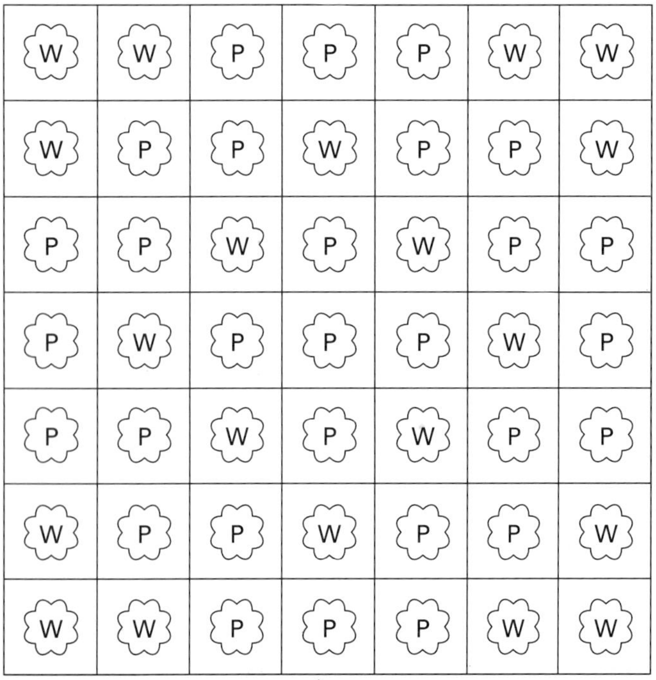

Diagram A

Border

Hold afghan with right-side facing you; join green in BL of 2nd hdc in upper right-hand corner.

Rnd 1:
Ch 3 (counts as a dc), 2 dc in same lp; † working in BLs only, dc in next 22 hdc, dc in next lp (used for joining), trc in joining, dc in next lp on next square (used for joining) †; rep from † to † 5 times more; dc in next 22 hdc, 3 dc in next hdc—corner made; * rep from † to † 6 times; dc in next 22 hdc, 3 dc in next hdc—corner made; rep from * once more; rep from † to † 6 times; dc in next 22 hdc; join in 3rd ch of beg ch-3.

Rnd 2:
Ch 1, sc in same ch as joining; ch 2, sk next st; * sc in next dc, ch 2, sk next st; rep from * around; join in first sc.

Rnd 3:
Sl st in next ch-2 sp, ch 1, in same sp work (sc, ch 2, sc)—corner made; ch 2; † sc in next ch-2 sp, ch 2 †; rep from † to † 85 times more; in next ch-2 sp work (sc, ch 2, sc)—corner made; ch 2; rep from † to † 85 times; in next ch-2 sp work (sc, ch 2, sc)—corner made; ch 2; rep from † to † 86 times; in next ch-2 sp work (sc, ch 2, sc)—corner made; ch 2; rep from † to † 85 times; join in first sc.

Rnds 4 through 7:
Rep Rnd 3.

Finish off and weave in ends.

Beautiful Dreams

Size:
About 35" x 48"

Materials:
Baby weight yarn, $10\frac{1}{2}$ oz (1785 yds, 315 g) ecru
Size D aluminum crochet hook, or size required for gauge

Gauge:
6 sc = 1"

Pattern Stitches

Cluster (CL):
Keeping last lp of each trc on hook, trc in st indicated, sk ch-3 sps indicated, trc in next st indicated, YO and draw through all 3 lps on hook—CL made.

Bobble:
Keeping last lp of each trc on hook, trc in st indicated, 4 trc in next st indicated; trc in next st indicated, YO and draw through all 7 lps on hook—bobble made.

Double Triple Crochet (dtrc):
YO 3 times, draw up lp in st indicated, (YO, draw through 2 lps on hook) 4 times—dtrc made.

Instructions

Ch 200 loosely.

Center

Row 1 (wrong side):
Sc in 2nd ch from hook; * ch 3, keeping last lp of each trc on hook, trc in same ch, sk next 5 chs, trc in next ch, YO and draw through all 3 lps on hook; ch 3, sc in same ch; rep from * 32 times more. Ch 4 (counts as first trc on following rows), turn.

Row 2 (right side):
Sk next ch-3 sp, in next st work (trc, ch 3, sc); * ch 3, CL (see Pattern Stitches) over same st, sk next 2 ch-3 sps, and over next st; ch 3, sc in same st; rep from * 31 times more; ch 3, CL over same st, sk next ch-3 sp, and over next sc. Ch 1, turn.

Row 3:
Sc in first CL, ch 3, CL over same CL and over next CL; ch 3, sc in same CL; * † ch 3, bobble (see Pattern Stitches) over same CL, over next sc, and over next CL; ch 3, sc in same CL †; ch 3, CL over same CL and next CL; ch 3, sc in same CL; rep from * 14 times more, then rep from † to † once; ch 3, CL over same CL and 4th ch of turning ch-4; ch 3, sc in same ch. Ch 4, turn.

Row 4:
Sk next ch-3 sp, in next CL work (trc, ch 3, sc); * ch 3, CL over same CL and next bobble; ch 3, sc in same bobble; ch 3, CL over same bobble and next CL; ch 3, sc in same CL; rep from * 15 times more; ch 3, CL over same CL and next sc. Ch 1, turn.

Row 5:
Sc in first CL; * ch 3, bobble over same CL, over next sc, and over next CL; ch 3, sc in same CL; ch 3, CL over same CL and next CL; ch 3, sc in same CL; rep from * 15 times more; ch 3, bobble over same CL, over next sc, and over 4th ch of turning ch-4; ch 3, sc in same ch. Ch 4, turn.

Rows 6 through 97:
Rep Rows 2 through 5 twenty-three times more.

Row 98:
Rep Row 2. At end of row, do not ch 1.

Finish off and weave in all ends.

Border

Hold center with right side facing you and Row 98 at top; join yarn in first ch-3 sp in upper right-hand corner.

Rnd 1:
Ch 3 (counts as a dc on this and following rnds), 4 dc in same sp—beg corner made; dc in next sc, 2 dc in next ch-3 sp; dc in next CL, (2 dc in next ch-3 sp, dc in next sc, 2 dc in next ch-3 sp, dc in next CL) 31 times; 2 dc in next ch-3 sp; dc in next sc, 5 dc in next ch-3 sp—corner made; working along next side, (4 dc in next sp, dc in ends of next 2 rows) 48 times; 4 dc in next sp; working along next side, 5 dc in next sp—corner made; (dc in unused lp of next ch, dc in next 5 skipped chs) 31 times; dc in unused lp of next ch, 5 dc in next sp—corner made; working along next side, (4 dc in next sp, dc in end of next 2 rows) 48 times; 4 dc in next sp; join in 3rd ch of beg ch-3—984 dc.

Rnd 2:
Ch 3, dc in next 5 dc, ch 2, sk next 2 dc; * dc in next 6 dc, ch 2, sk next 2 dc; rep from * around; join in 3rd ch of beg ch-3.

Rnd 3:
Sl st in next 5 dc and in next ch-2 sp; ch 5; † YO 3 times, insert hook in same sp and draw lp through, (YO, draw through 2 lps on hook) 3 times †; rep from † to † once

continued on page 21

more; YO and draw through all 3 lps on hook—beg dtrc cluster made; (ch 6, dc in 6th ch from hook) 3 times; rep from † to † 3 times; YO and draw through all 4 lps on hook—dtrc cluster made; †† in next ch-2 sp work [dtrc cluster, (ch 6, dc in 6th ch from hook) 3 times; dtrc cluster] ††; rep from †† to †† 23 times more; (ch 6, dc in 6th ch from hook) 3 times; rep from †† to †† 37 times; (ch 6, dc in 6th ch from hook) 3 times; rep from †† to †† 24 times; (ch 6, dc in 6th ch from hook) 3 times; rep from †† to †† 37 times; join in beg dtrc cluster.

Rnd 4:
Sl st in next 2 chs of next ch-5 sp, ch 1, sc in same sp; ch 5, sc in next ch-5 sp, ch 5; * dec over next 2 ch-5 sps (to work dec: draw up lp in each of next 2 ch-5 sps, YO and draw through all 3 lps on hook—dec made); ch 5, sc in next ch-5 sp, ch 5; rep from * to last ch-5 sp; sc in last ch-5 sp; join in first sc.

Rnd 5:
Ch 1, sc in same sc; (ch 5, sc in next sc) 50 times; † ch 5, sc in next sc, ch 7, dc in 6th ch from hook, dc in sc just made; sc in same sc on Rnd 4 †; (ch 5, sc in next sc) 75 times; rep from † to † once; (ch 5, sc in next sc) 49 times; rep from † to † once; (ch 5, sc in next sc) 75 times; rep from † to † once; ch 5; join in first sc.

Rnd 6:
Ch 1, sc in same sc; (ch 5, sc in next sc) 51 times; ch 9, sc in next sc, (ch 5, sc in next sc) 76 times; ch 9, sc in next sc, (ch 5, sc in next sc) 50 times; ch 9, sc in next sc, (ch 5, sc in next sc) 76 times; ch 9, sc in next sc, ch 5; join in first sc.

Rnd 7:
Ch 1, sc in same sc; (ch 6, sc in next sc) 51 times; ch 11, sc in next sc, (ch 6, sc in next sc) 76 times; ch 11, sc in next sc, (ch 6, sc in next sc) 50 times; ch 11, sc in next sc, (ch 6, sc in next sc) 76 times; ch 11, sc in next sc, ch 6; join in first sc. Finish off.

Rnd 8:
Make lp on hook and join with an sc over ch sps of Rnds 4 through 7 to right of rnd joinings; † ch 8, dtrc (see Pattern Stitches on page 19) in 8th ch from hook, sc over ch sps of Rnds 4 through 7 †; rep from † to † 50 times more; ch 3, sc in next sc, ch 11, sc in next sc, ch 3, sc over ch sps of Rnds 4 through 7; rep from † to † 75 times; ch 3, sc in next sc, ch 11, sc in next sc, ch 3, sc over ch sps of Rnds 4 through 7; rep from † to † 49 times; ch 3, sc in next sc, ch 11, sc in next sc, ch 3, sc over ch sps of Rnds 4 through 7; rep from † to † 75 times; ch 3, sc in next sc, ch 11, sc in next sc, ch 3; join in first sc.

Finish off and weave in ends.

Blue Ribbon Baby

Size:
About 35" x 42"

Materials:
Baby weight yarn, 10½ oz (1785 yds, 315 g) blue
Size D aluminum crochet hook, or size required for gauge

Gauge:
6 dc = 1"

Pattern Stitch

Cluster (CL):
Keeping last lp of each dc on hook, 3 dc in sp indicated; YO and draw through all 4 lps on hook—CL made.

Instructions

Ch 205 loosely.

Center

Row 1 (right side):
In 5th ch from hook work (dc, ch 1) twice (beg 4 skipped chs count as a dc and a ch-1 sp); sk next 4 chs, sc in next ch, ch 1, sk next 4 chs; * in next ch work (dc, ch 1) 6 times; sk next 4 chs, sc in next ch, ch 1, sk next 4 chs; rep from * 18 times more; in last ch work (dc, ch 1) twice; dc in same ch. Ch 1, turn.

Row 2:
Sc in first dc, ch 3, in next sc work (dc, ch 3, dc); ch 3; * sk next 3 dc, sc in next ch-1 sp, ch 3, in next sc work (dc, ch 3, dc); ch 3; rep from * 18 times more; sk next 2 dc and next ch of beg 4 skipped chs, sc in next ch. Ch 1, turn.

Row 3:
Sc in first sc, ch 2, sk next ch-3 sp, in next ch-3 sp work [CL(see Pattern Stitch) ch 2] 3 times; sk next dc, sc in next sc; * ch 2, sk next ch-3 sp, in next ch-3 sp work (CL, ch 2) 3 times; sk next dc, sc in next sc; rep from * across. Ch 7 (counts as first dc and ch-4 sp on following rows), turn.

Row 4:
Sk first CL, sc in next CL, ch 4, dc in next sc; * ch 4, sk next CL, sc in next CL, ch 4, dc in next sc; rep from * across. Ch 4 (counts as first dc and ch-1 sp on following rows), turn.

Row 5:
In first dc work (dc, ch 1) twice; sc in next sc, ch 1; * in next dc work (dc, ch 1) 6 times; sc in next sc, ch 1; rep from * across to turning ch-7; sk next 4 chs of turning ch-7, in next ch work (dc, ch 1) twice; dc in same ch. Ch 1, turn.

Row 6:
Sc in first dc, ch 3, in next sc work (dc, ch 3, dc); ch 3; * sk next 3 dc, sc in next ch-1 sp, ch 3, in next sc work (dc, ch 3, dc); ch 3; rep from * 18 times more; sk next 2 dc and next ch of turning ch-4, sc in next ch. Ch 1, turn.

Rows 7 through 130:
Rep Rows 3 through 6 thirty-one times more.

Rows 131 and 132:
Rep Rows 3 and 4. At end of Row 132, do not ch 4.

Finish off and weave in all ends.

Border

Hold center with right side facing you and Row 132 at top; join yarn in ch-4 sp in upper right-hand corner.

Rnd 1:
Ch 1, 4 sc in same sp; * sc in next sc, 3 sc in next ch-4 sp; sc in next dc, 3 sc in next ch-4 sp; rep from * 18 times more; 2 sc in next sc; 7 sc in sp formed by turning ch-7; working along next side in ends of rows and in sps formed by edge dc and turning chs, ** sc in next 2 rows, 2 sc in next sp; 3 sc in next sp; rep from ** 31 times more; sc in next 2 rows, 2 sc in next sp; working along next side in sps formed by skipped chs and in unused lps of chs, 7 sc in next sp; *** sc in next unused lp, 3 sc in next sp; rep from *** 37 times more; 2 sc in next unused lp; 7 sc in next sp; working along next side in ends of rows and in sp formed by edge dc and turning chs, 2 sc in sp formed by beg 4 skipped chs of beg ch-205; **** sc in next 2 rows, 3 sc in next sp; 2 sc in next sp; rep from **** 31 times more; sc in next 2 rows; join in first sc—792 sc.

Rnd 2:
Ch 6 (counts as a dc and a ch-3 sp), sk next 3 sc; * dc in next sc, ch 3, sk next 3 sc; rep from * around; join in 3rd ch of beg ch-6—198 dc.

continued on page 24

Rnd 3:
Ch 4 **(**counts as a trc on this and following rnds**)**, in same ch as joining work **(**2 trc, ch 3, 3 trc**)**; ch 2, sc in next dc, ch 2; * in next dc work **(**3 trc, ch 3, 3 trc**)**; ch 2, sc in next dc, ch 2; rep from * around; join in 4th ch of beg ch-4.

Rnd 4:
Sl st in next 2 trc and in next ch-3 sp, ch 1, sc in same sp; ch 5, sk next ch-2 sp, sc in next sc, ch 5, sk next ch-2 sp; * sc in next ch-3 sp, ch 5, sk next ch-2 sp, sc in next sc, ch 5, sk next ch-2 sp; rep from * around; join in first sc.

Rnd 5:
Ch 1, sc in same sc; ch 4; * sc in next sc, ch 4; rep from * around; join in first sc.

Rnd 6:
Ch 4, in same sc work **(**2 trc, ch 3, 3 trc**)**; ch 3, sc in next sc, ch 3; * in next sc work **(**3 trc, ch 3**)** twice; sc in next sc, ch 3; rep from * around; join in 4th ch of beg ch-4.

Rnd 7:
Ch 1, sc in same ch as joining and in next 2 trc; ch 3, dc in 3rd ch from hook, sc in next 3 trc, 3 sc in next ch-3 sp; sc in next sc, 3 sc in next ch-3 sp; * sc in next 3 trc, ch 3, dc in 3rd ch from hook, sc in next 3 trc, 3 sc in next ch-3 sp; sc in next sc, 3 sc in next ch-3 sp; rep from * around; join in first sc.

Rnd 8:
* Sl st in next sc, ch 3, sk next sc, in next ch-3 sp work **(**sl st, ch 3**)** twice; sk next sc, **(**sl st in next sc, ch 3, sk next sc**)** twice; draw up lp in next sc, sk next sc, draw up lp in next sc, YO and draw through all 3 lps on hook; ch 3, sk next sc, sl st in next sc, ch 3, sk next sc; rep from * around; join in first sl st.

Finish off and weave in ends.

Buttercup for Baby

Size:
About 39" x 47"

Materials:
Baby weight yarn, 15 oz (2550 yds, 450 g) yellow
Size D aluminum crochet hook, or size required for gauge

Gauge:
6 sc = 1"
6 sc rows = 1"

Pattern Stitches

Puff Stitch (puff st):
YO, insert hook in sp indicated, draw lp through, (YO, insert hook in same sp, draw lp through) twice; YO and draw through all 7 lps on hook; ch 1—puff st made.

Beginning Cluster (beg CL):
Ch 4, keeping last lp of each trc on hook, 3 trc in sp indicated; YO and draw through all 4 lps on hook—beg CL made.

Cluster (CL):
Keeping last lp of each trc on hook, 4 trc in sp indicated; YO and draw through all 5 lps on hook—CL made.

Instructions

Ch 224 loosely.

Center

Row 1 (right side):
Sc in 9th from hook, ch 1, sk next ch, sc in next ch; * ch 3, sk next 2 chs, dc in next ch, ch 1, sk next ch, dc in next ch, ch 3, sk next 2 chs, sc in next ch, ch 1, sk next ch, sc in next ch; rep from * 20 times more; ch 3, sk next 2 chs, dc in next ch. Ch 1, turn.

Row 2:
Sc in first dc; * † ch 3, sk next ch-3 sp, in next ch-1 sp work [puff st (see Pattern Stitches), ch 2] twice; puff st in same sp; ch 3 †; sk next ch-3 sp, sc in next ch-1 sp; rep from * 20 times more, then rep from † to † once; sk next 3 chs of beg 8 skipped chs, sc in next ch. Ch 1, turn.

Row 3:
Sc in first sc, ch 3, sk next ch-3 sp; * † dc in next ch-2 sp, ch 1, dc in next ch-2 sp, ch 3 †; sc in next ch-3 sp, ch 1, sc in next ch-3 sp, ch 3; rep from * 20 times more, then rep from † to † once; sc in next sc. Ch 6 (counts as first dc and ch-3 sp on following rows), turn.

Row 4:
Sk next ch-3 sp, sc in next ch-1 sp; * ch 3, sk next ch-3 sp, in next ch-1 sp work (puff st, ch 2) twice; puff st in same sp; ch 3, sk next ch-3 sp, sc in next ch-1 sp; rep from * 20 times more; ch 3, dc in next sc. Ch 6, turn.

Row 5:
Sc in next ch-3 sp; * ch 1, sc in next ch-3 sp, ch 3, dc in next ch-2 sp, ch 1, dc in next ch-2 sp, ch 3, sc in next ch-3 sp; rep from * 20 times more; ch 1, sc in ch-3 sp formed by first 3 chs of turning ch-6, ch 3, dc in next ch. Ch 1, turn.

Row 6:
Sc in first dc; * † ch 3, sk next ch-3 sp, in next ch-1 sp work (puff st, ch 2) twice; puff st in same sp; ch 3 †; sk next ch-3 sp, sc in next ch-1 sp; rep from * 20 times more, then rep from † to † once; sk next 3 chs of turning ch-6, sc in next ch. Ch 1, turn.

Rows 7 through 154:
Rep Rows 3 through 6 thirty-seven times more.

Rows 155 through 157:
Rep Rows 3 through 5. At end of Row 157, do not ch 1.

Finish off and weave in all ends.

Border

Rnd 1:
Hold center with right side facing you and Row 157 at top; join yarn in ch-6 sp in upper right-hand corner; ch 1, 10 sc in same sp; * sc in next sc, in next ch-1 sp, and in next sc; 2 sc in next ch-3 sp; sc in next dc, in next ch-1 sp, and in next dc; 2 sc in next ch-3 sp; rep from * 20 times more; sc in next sc, in next ch-1 sp, and in next sc; 10 sc in lp formed by next ch 3 and next dc; working along next side in sps formed by turning chs and in ends of rows, ** 3 sc in next sp; sc in next 2 rows, 2 sc in next sp; rep from ** 37 times more; 3 sc in next sp; sc in next 2 rows; 10 sc in lp formed by last 3 chs of beg ch and last dc of Row 1; working in unused lps of beg chs and in sps formed by skipped chs, *** sc in next lp, in next sp, and in next lp; 2 sc in next sp; sc in next lp, in next sp, and in next lp; 2 sc in next sp; rep from *** 20 times more; sc in next lp, in next sp, and in next lp; 10 sc in lp formed by beg 8 skipped chs; working along next side in sps formed by turning chs and in ends of rows, sc in next 2 rows; **** 3 sc in next sp; 2 sc in next sp; sc in next 2 rows; rep from **** 37 times more; 3 sc in next sp; join in first sc—1008 sc.

continued on page 27

Rnd 2:
Ch 1, sc in same sc; ch 3, sk next 3 sc; * sc in next sc, ch 3, sk next 3 sc; rep from * around; join in first sc—252 ch-3 sps.

Rnd 3:
Sl st in next ch-3 sp, ch 1, sc in same sp; ch 3; * sc in next ch-3 sp, ch 3; rep from * around; join in first sc.

Rnd 4:
Ch 1, sc in same sc; 3 sc in next ch-3 sp; sc in next sc; * ch 6, sc in next sc, 3 sc in next ch-3 sp; sc in next sc; rep from * to last ch-3 sp; ch 2; join with a trc in first sc.

Rnd 5:
Beg CL (see Pattern Stitches on page 25) in sp formed by joining trc; ch 3, in same sp work [CL (see Pattern Stitches on page 25), ch 3, CL]; ch 4, sc in next ch-6 sp, ch 4; * in next ch-6 sp work (CL, ch 3) twice; CL in same sp; ch 4, sc in next ch-6 sp, ch 4; rep from * around; join in beg CL—sixty-three 3-CL groups.

Rnd 6:
Sl st in next ch-3 sp, beg CL in same sp; * † ch 3, CL in next ch-3 sp; ch 3, CL in next ch-4 sp; ch 3, trc in next sc, ch 3, CL in next ch-4 sp; ch 3 †; CL in next ch-3 sp; rep from * 61 times more, then rep from † to † once; join in beg CL.

Rnd 7:
Sl st in next ch-3 sp, ch 3 (counts as a dc on this and following rnds), 3 dc in same sp; ch 3, (sc in next ch-3 sp, ch 3) 4 times; * 4 dc in next ch-3 sp; ch 3, (sc in next ch-3 sp, ch 3) 4 times; rep from * around; join in 3rd ch of beg ch-3.

Rnd 8:
Sl st in next dc, ch 3, dc in next dc, ch 3, (sc in next ch-3 sp, ch 3) 5 times; sk next dc; * dc in next 2 dc, ch 3, (sc in next ch-3 sp, ch 3) 5 times; sk next dc; rep from * around; join in 3rd ch of beg ch-3.

Rnd 9:
Ch 1, sc in same ch as joining; ch 3, sc in next dc, 3 sc in each of next 6 ch-3 sps; * sc in next dc, ch 3, sc in next dc, 3 sc in each of next 6 ch-3 sps; rep from * around; join in first sc.

Rnd 10:
Sl st in next ch-3 sp, ch 1, in same sp work (sc, ch 2, puff st, ch 2, sc); ch 3, sk next 2 sc, (sc in next sc, ch 3, sk next 2 sc) 6 times; * in next ch-3 sp work (sc, ch 2, puff st, ch 2, sc); ch 3, sk next 2 sc, (sc in next sc, ch 3, sk next 2 sc) 6 times; rep from * around; join in first sc.

Finish off and weave in ends.

Bright Crayons

Size:
About 36" x 44"

Materials:
Sport weight yarn, 6 oz (570 yds, 180 g) each, dk blue and lt blue; 5 oz (475 yds, 150 g) yellow; 2 oz (190 yds, 60 g) pink
Size 7, 36" circular knitting needle, or size required for gauge

Gauge:
9 sts = 2" in stockinette stitch (knit one row, purl one row)

Instructions

With pink, cast on 192 sts.

Row 1 ((wrong side)**:**
Purl.

Row 2 (right side)**:**
Knit.

Row 3:
Purl.

Row 4:
* (K2 tog tbl) twice; (YO, K1) 4 times; (K2 tog tbl) twice; rep from * 15 times more.

Row 5:
Knit.

Rows 6 through 9:
Join dk blue, cut pink; rep Rows 2 through 5.

Rows 10 through 17:
Join lt blue, cut dk blue; rep Rows 2 through 5 twice.

Rows 18 through 21:
Join dk blue, cut lt blue; rep Rows 2 through 5.

Rows 22 through 29:
Join lt blue, cut dk blue; rep Rows 2 through 5 twice.

Rows 30 through 33:
Join dk blue, cut lt blue; rep Rows 2 through 5.

Rows 34 through 49:
Join yellow, cut dk blue; rep Rows 2 through 5 four times.

Rows 50 through 53:
Join dk blue, cut yellow; rep Rows 2 through 5.

Rows 54 through 57:
Join pink, cut dk blue; rep Rows 2 through 5.

Rows 58 through 61:
Join dk blue, cut pink; rep Rows 2 through 5.

Rows 62 through 77:
Rep Rows 34 through 49.

Rows 78 through 81:
Join dk blue, cut yellow; rep Rows 2 through 5.

Rows 82 through 105:
Rep Rows 10 through 33.

Rows 106 through 313:
Join pink, cut dk blue; rep Rows 2 through 105 twice.

Rows 314 through 316:
Join pink, cut dk blue; rep Rows 2 through 4.

Bind off as to knit.

CRAYON
CRAYON
CRAYON

Rings of Love

Size:
About 33" x 42"

Materials:
Worsted weight yarn, 17 oz (1190 yds, 510 g) white; $2\frac{1}{2}$ oz (175 yds, 75 g) each, blue, red, yellow, and green
Size G aluminum crochet hook, or size required for gauge
Size 16 tapestry needle

Gauge:
4 sc = 1"
motif = $3\frac{1}{2}$" x $3\frac{1}{2}$"

Instructions

Motif (make 80)

First Ring:
With blue, ch 10; join to form a ring. Finish off.

Second Ring:
With red, ch 10; slip beg end through first ring (see **Fig 1**); join in first ch. Finish off.

Fig 1

Third Ring:
With yellow, ch 10; slip beg end under first ring, over intersection of first and second rings and under second ring (see **Fig 2**); join in first ch. Finish off.

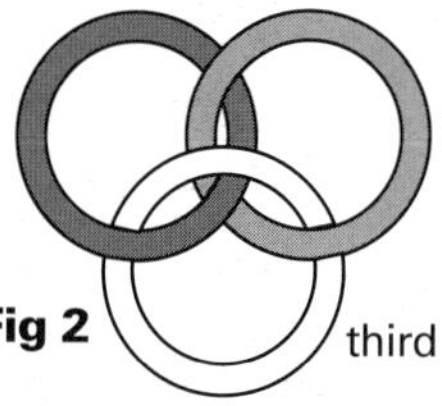

Fig 2

Fourth Ring:
With green, ch 10; slip beg end under first ring, over intersection of first and second ring (beside third ring) and under second ring (see **Fig 3**); join in first ch. Finish off.

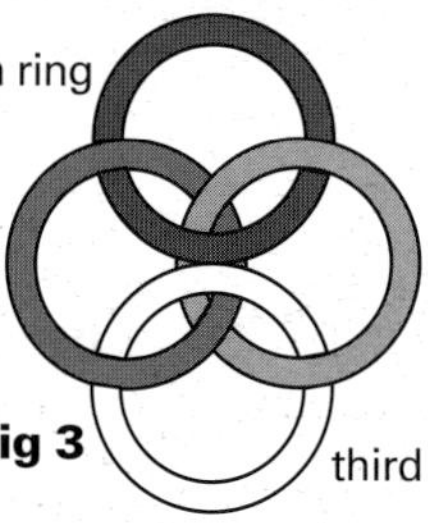

Fig 3

Motif Border:
With white, make lp on hook and join with an sc in first (blue) ring.

Rnd 1 (right side):
Ch 2, sc in same ring; ch 2, sc over intersection of first ring and fourth ring (see **Fig 4**), ch 2; in fourth ring work (sc, ch 2) twice; sc over intersection of fourth ring and second ring, ch 2; in second ring work (sc, ch 2) twice; sc over intersection of second ring and third ring, ch 2; in third ring work (sc, ch 2) twice; sc over intersection of third ring and first ring, ch 2; join in joining sc—12 sc and 12 ch-2 sps.

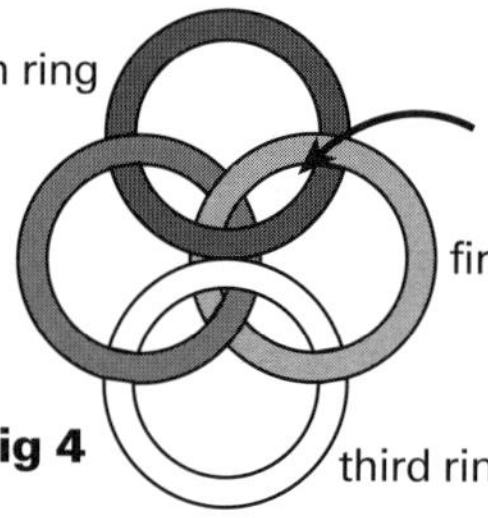

Fig 4

Rnd 2:
Ch 1, sc in same sc; * in next ch-2 sp work (sc, ch 2, sc)—corner made; sc in next sc, in next ch-2 sp, in next sc, in next ch-2 sp, and in next sc; rep from * twice more; in next ch-2 sp work (sc, ch 2, sc)—corner made; sc in next sc, in next ch-2 sp, in next sc, and in next ch-2 sp; join in first sc—28 sc and 4 ch-2 sps. Finish off.

Note: Make 20 motifs using blue for Rnd 3; make 20 motifs using red for Rnd 3; make 20 motifs using yellow for Rnd 3; and make 20 motifs using green for Rnd 3.

Rnd 3:
Make lp on hook and join with an sc in any corner ch-2 sp; ch 3, sc in same sp—corner made; * sc in next 7 sc, in next corner ch-2 sp work (sc, ch 3, sc)—corner made; rep from * twice more; sc in next 7 sc; join in joining sc. Finish off.

Rnd 4:
With white, make lp on hook and join with an sc in first sc after any corner ch-3 sp; sc in next 8 sc; * † working behind corner ch-3 sp of prev rnd, in corner ch-2 sp of Rnd 2 work (dc, ch 3, dc)—corner made †; on working rnd, sc in next 9 sc; rep from * twice more, then rep from † to † once; join in joining sc.

Finish off and weave in all ends.

continued on page 32

Rings of Love

Square (make 20)
Each square is made up of 4 motifs (one of each color). Refer to **Diagram A** for color placement. To join motifs, hold 2 motifs with wrong sides together carefully matching sts and being sure all rings are in the same position. With tapestry needle and white and beg and ending with 2nd ch of each corner, sew with overcast st (see Stitch Guide on page 5) through back lps only. Join rem 2 motifs together in same manner. Then join both pieces together, being sure that all corner junctions are firmly joined. Join rem motifs into squares in same manner.

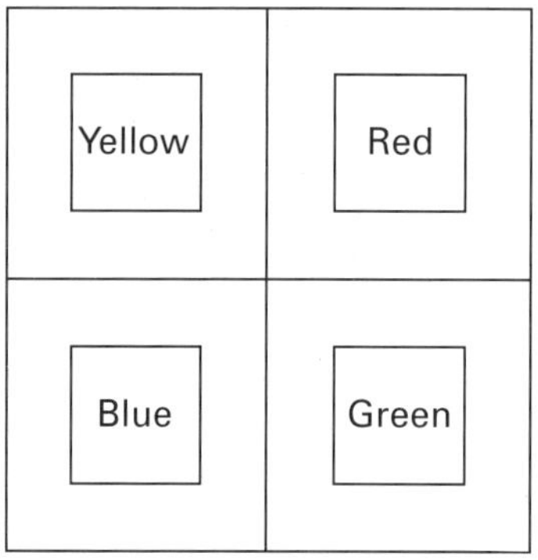

Diagram A

Square Edging
Hold joined motifs with right side facing you; with white, make lp on hook and join with an sc in any outer corner ch-3 sp.

Rnd 1 (right side):
Ch 2, sc in same sp—beg corner made; working in BLs only, * † sc in next 11 sc, hdc in next ch, in motif joining, and in next ch; sc in next 11 sc †; in next corner ch-3 sp work (sc, ch 2, sc)—corner made; rep from * twice more, then rep from † to † once; join in joining sc. Finish off.

Note: Make 4 squares using blue for Rnd 2; make 4 squares using red for Rnd 2; make 6 squares using yellow for Rnd 2; and make 6 squares using green for Rnd 2.

Rnd 2:
Make lp on hook and join with an sc in any corner ch-2 sp; ch 3, sc in same sp—beg corner made; sc in next 27 sts; * in next corner ch-2 sp work (sc, ch 3, sc)—corner made; sc in next 27 sts; rep from * twice more; join in joining sc. Finish off.

Rnd 3:
With white, make lp on hook and join with an sc in first sc after any corner ch-3 sp; sc in next 28 sc; * † working behind corner ch-3 sp of prev rnd, in corner ch-2 sp of Rnd 1 work (dc, ch 3, dc)—corner made †; on working rnd, sc in next 29 sc; rep from * twice more, then rep from † to † once; join in joining sc.

Assembly
Join squares together referring to **Diagram B** for color placement and making sure all squares have motifs in same position. To join squares, hold 2 squares with wrong sides together carefully matching sts. With tapestry needle and white and beg and ending with 2nd ch of each corner, sew with overcast st (see Stitch Guide on page 5) through back lps only. Join rem squares together in same manner, being sure that all corner junctions are firmly joined.

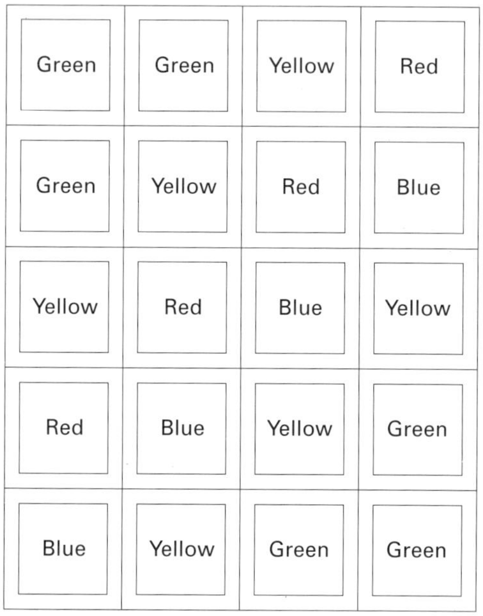

Diagram B

Border
Hold afghan with right side facing you and one short end at top.

Rnd 1 (right side):
With white, make lp on hook and join with an sc in ch-3 sp in upper right-hand corner, ch 3, sc in same sp—beg corner made; working in BLs only, † sc in next 31 sts; hdc in next ch, in square joining, and in next ch †; rep from † to † twice more; sc in next 31 sts; in next corner ch-3 sp work (sc, ch 3, sc); rep from † to † 4 times; sc in next 31 sts; in next corner ch-3 sp work (sc, ch 3, sc); rep from † to † 3 times; sc in next 31 sts; in next corner ch-3 sp work (sc, ch 3, sc); rep from † to † 4 times; sc in next 31 sts; join in first sc.

Rnd 2:
Ch 1, sc in same sc; * † in next ch-3 sp work (sc, ch 3, sc)—corner made †; sc in each st to next corner ch-3 sp; rep from * twice more; then rep from † to † once; sc in each st to first sc; join in first sc.

Finish off and weave in all ends.

Little Angel
Lavender and Lace

Rosebuds for Baby
Lullaby and Goodnight

Kitty Cat Lullaby

Sweetheart Mile-a-Minute

So Pretty

Rock-a-Bye Baby

Beautiful Dreams

Baby
Peach Blossom
Buttercup
for Baby

Pink
Roses
Bundles
of Joy

Blue Ribbon Baby
Baby Seashells

Rainbow Sprinkles
CRAYON
Bright Crayons

So Pretty

Size:
About 35" x 45" including border

Materials:
Baby weight yarn, 8½ oz (1445 yds, 255 g) baby pink; 4 oz (680 yds, 120 g) white
Size 4, 36" circular knitting needle, or size required for gauge (for afghan center)
Size 4, straight knitting needles, or size required for gauge (for border)
Size 16 tapestry needle

Gauge:
7 sts = 1" in stockinette stitch (knit one row, purl one row)
8 rows = 1"

Instructions

Body

With pink, cast on 237 sts.

Row 1 (wrong side)**:**
* (K3, P1) twice; K1, P1; rep from * across to last 7 sts; K3, P1, K3.

Row 2 (right side)**:**
* (P3, K1) twice; P1, K1; rep from * across to last 7 sts; P3, K1, P3.

Row 3:
K2, P1, K1, P1; * (K3, P1) twice; K1, P1; rep from * across to last 2 sts; K2.

Row 4:
P2, K1, P1, K1; * (P3, K1) twice; P1, K1; rep from * across to last 2 sts; P2.

Row 5:
(K1, P1) 3 times; * (K2, P1) twice; (K1, P1) twice; rep from * across to last st; K1.

Row 6:
(P1, K1) 3 times; * (P2, K1) twice; (P1, K1) twice; rep from * across to last st; P1.

Rows 7 and 8:
Rep Rows 3 and 4.

Rows 9 and 10:
Rep Rows 1 and 2.

Row 11:
K3, P1; * K2, (P1, K1) twice; P1, K2, P1; rep from * across to last 3 sts; K3.

Row 12:
P3, K1; * P2, (K1, P1) twice; K1, P2, K1; rep from * across to last 3 sts; P3.

Rows 13 through 348:
Rep Rows 1 through 12, twenty-eight times more.

Bind off.

Border

Edging:
With white, cast on 17 sts.

Note: Increases are made by knitting into the front and back of the same stitch.

Row 1 (right side)**:**
K2, YO, K3, YO, K2 tog; (P1, K1) 4 times; P1, inc—19 sts.

Note: On following rows, slip stitches as if to knit.

Row 2:
Sl 1, K2 tog; (K1, P1) 3 times; K1, K2 tog; YO, K5, YO, K2.

Row 3:
K2, YO, K1, K2 tog; YO, K1, YO, K2 tog; K1, YO, K2 tog; (P1, K1) 3 times; P1, inc—21 sts.

Row 4:
Sl 1, K2 tog; (K1, P1) twice; K1, (K2 tog, YO, K1) twice; K2, YO, K2 tog; K1, YO, K2.

Row 5:
K2, YO, K1, K2 tog; YO, K5, YO, K2 tog; K1, YO, K2 tog; (P1, K1) twice; P1, inc—23 sts.

Row 6:
Sl 1, K2 tog; K1, P1, K1; (K2 tog, YO, K1) twice; K6, YO, K2 tog; K1, YO, K2.

Row 7:
(K2 tog, K1, YO) twice; K2 tog; K3, (K2 tog, YO, K1) twice; (P1, K1) twice; P1, inc.

Row 8:
Sl 1, K2 tog; (K1, P1) 3 times; YO, K2 tog; K1, YO, K2 tog; (K1, K2 tog, YO) twice; K1, K2 tog—21 sts.

Row 9:
(K2 tog, K1, YO) twice; K3 tog; YO, K1, K2 tog; YO, (K1, P1) 4 times; inc.

Row 10:
Sl 1, K2 tog; (K1, P1) 4 times; YO, K2 tog; K3, K2 tog; YO, K1, K2 tog—19 sts.

continued on page 39

Row 11:
K2 tog; K1, YO, K2 tog; K1, K2 tog; YO, (K1, P1) 5 times; inc.

Row 12:
Sl 1, K2 tog; (K1, P1) 5 times; YO, K3 tog; YO, K1, K2 tog—17 sts.

Rep Rows 1 through 12 of edging 29 times more for one short edge.

Corner:
Note: Corner is worked in short rows.

Row 1(right side):
K2, YO, K3, YO, K2 tog; P1, K1. Turn, leaving rem 8 sts unworked.

Row 2:
K1, K2 tog; YO, K5, YO, K2—19 sts.

Row 3:
K2, YO, K1, K2 tog; YO, K1, YO, K2 tog; K1, YO, K2 tog; P1. Turn, leaving rem 7 sts unworked.

Row 4:
(K2 tog, YO, K1) twice; K2, YO, K2 tog; K1, YO, K2—21 sts.

Row 5:
K2, YO, K1, K2 tog; YO, K5, YO, K2 tog; K1, YO, K2 tog; P1. Turn, leaving rem 5 sts unworked.

Row 6:
(K2 tog, YO, K1) twice; K6, YO, K2 tog; K1, YO, K2—23 sts.

Row 7:
(K2 tog, K1, YO) twice; K2 tog; K3, (K2 tog, YO, K1) twice. Turn, leaving rem 6 sts unworked.

Row 8:
K1, P1, YO, K2 tog; K1, YO, K2 tog; (K1, K2 tog, YO) twice; K1, K2 tog—21 sts.

Row 9:
(K2 tog, K1, YO) twice; K3 tog; YO, K1, K2 tog; YO, K1, P1. Turn, leaving rem 7 sts unworked.

Row 10:
P1, K1, P1, YO, K2 tog; K3, K2 tog; YO, K1, K2 tog—19 sts.

Row 11:
K2 tog; K1, YO, K2 tog; K1, K2 tog; YO, (K1, P1) 5 times; inc.

Note: Mark beg of Rnd 12.

Row 12:
Sl 1, K2 tog; (K1, P1) 5 times; YO, K3 tog; YO, K1, K2 tog—17 sts.

Rep Rows 1 through 12 of corner twice more.

Rep Rows 1 through 12 of edging 36 times for one long side.

Rep Rows 1 through 12 of corner 3 times.

Rep Rows 1 through 12 of edging 30 times for one short side.

Rep Rows 1 through 12 of corner 3 times.

Rep Rows 1 through 12 of edging 36 times for one long side.

Rep Rows 1 through 12 of corner 3 times.

Bind off.

Finishing

Hold border with first and last rows with right sides together. Sew edges together.

Pin right side of border to right side of afghan center, matching corners and sides and easing as necessary. Sew border in place.

Bundles of Joy

Size:
About 36" x 42" without fringe

Materials:
Sport weight yarn, 15 oz (1425 yds, 450 g) blue;
5 oz (475 yds, 150 g) white
Size 6, 36" circular knitting needle, or size required for gauge

Gauge:
5 sts = 1" in stockinette stitch (knit one row, purl one row)

Note: Yarn is carried along edge of afghan. When changing to a new color at the beginning of the row, bring the new color under the old color. When carrying the old color along edge, bring the working color under the old color at the beginning of the row, to lock it in place.

Instructions

With blue, cast on 185 sts.

Row 1 (right side)**:**
Knit.

Row 2:
Purl. Drop blue.

Row 3:
Join white, K4; * yf, sl 3 as to purl, yb, K3; rep from * to last st; K1.

Row 4:
P4; * yb, sl 3 as to purl, yf, P3; rep from * to last st; P1. Drop white.

Row 5:
With blue, knit.

Row 6:
Purl.

Row 7:
K5; * insert right needle under 2 strands of white and into next st as to knit, knit st and bring strands over needle, K5; rep from * across.

Row 8:
Purl. Drop blue.

Row 9:
With white, K1; * yf, sl 3 as to purl, yb, K3; rep from * to last 4 sts; yf, sl 3 as to purl, yb, K1.

Row 10:
P1; * yb, sl 3 as to purl, yf, P3; rep from * to last 4 sts; yb, sl 3 as to purl, yf, P1. Drop white.

Row 11:
With blue, knit.

Row 12:
Purl.

Row 13:
K2; * insert right needle under 2 strands of white and into next st, knit st and bring strands over the needle; K5; rep from * to last 3 sts, insert right needle under 2 strands of white and into next st, knit the st and bring strands over the needle, K2.

Row 14:
Purl. Drop blue.

Rows 15 through 362:
Rep Rows 3 through 14 twenty-nine times more.

Rows 363 through 368:
Rep Rows 3 through 7.

Bind off as to purl.

Fringe

Following Fringe Instructions on page 6, make Single Knot Fringe. Cut 20" strands; use 6 strands for each knot. Tie knots evenly spaced (about every $^1/_2$") across cast on edge only of afghan, to avoid having fringe close to baby's face.

Sweetheart Mile-a-Minute

Size:
About 38" x 44"

Materials:
Sport weight yarn, 4 oz (380 yds, 120 g) each, white, pink, and blue
Size G aluminum crochet hook, or size required for gauge

Gauge:
4 dc = 1"

Pattern Stitch

Cluster (CL):
Keeping last lp of each dc on hook, 2 dc in st indicated; YO and draw through all 3 lps on hook—CL made.

Instructions

Panel

Strip Center (make 6 blue and 5 pink):
Ch 8.

Row 1 (right side):
Sc in 2nd ch from hook, ch 1, sk next 2 chs, in next ch work [CL (see Pattern Stitch), ch 2, CL, ch 2, CL]; ch 1, sk next 2 chs, sc in next ch. Ch 3 (counts as first dc on following rows), turn.

Row 2:
Dc in first sc, ch 2, sk next CL, sc in next CL, ch 2, 2 dc in next sc. Ch 5 (counts as first dc and ch-2 sp on following rows), turn.

Row 3:
CL in first dc; ch 1, sc in next sc, ch 1, in 3rd ch of turning ch-3 work (CL, ch 2, dc). Ch 1, turn.

Row 4:
Sc in first dc, ch 2, 3 dc in next sc; ch 2, sk next 2 chs of turning ch-5, sc in next ch. Ch 1, turn.

Row 5:
Sc in first sc, ch 1, in 2nd dc of next 3-dc group work (CL, ch 2, CL, ch 2, CL); ch 1, sc in next sc. Ch 3, turn.

Rows 6 through 101:
Rep Rows 2 through 5 twenty-four times more.

At end of Row 101, do not ch 3; do not turn.

Strip Border:

Rnd 1:
2 sc in same sc as last sc made; working along edge in edge sc and sps formed by edge dc, 2 sc in each of next 2 rows; * sc in each of next 2 rows, 2 sc in each of next 2 rows; rep from * 23 times more; sc in next row; working in unused lps of beg ch, 3 sc in next lp—corner made; sc in next ch-2 sp, 3 sc in next lp; sc in next ch-2 sp, 3 sc in next lp—corner made; working along next edge in edge sc and in sps formed by edge dc, sc in next row; ** 2 sc in each of next 2 rows; sc in each of next 2 rows; rep from ** 23 times more; 2 sc in each of next 3 rows; working across Row 101, 3 sc in first sc—corner made; sc in next CL, in next ch-2 sp, in next CL, in next ch-2 sp and in next CL; 3 sc in next sc—corner made; join in first sc. Finish off.

Rnd 2:
Join white in 2nd sc in upper left-hand corner; ch 2, in same sc work (dc, ch 2, CL, ch 2, CL)—corner made; working along side, † sk next 2 sc, in next sc work (CL, ch 1, CL) †; rep from † to † 49 times more; sk next 3 sc, in next sc work (CL, ch 2, CL, ch 2, CL)—corner made; †† sk next sc, in next sc work (CL, ch 1, CL) ††; rep from †† to †† twice more; sk next sc, in next sc work (CL, ch 2, CL, ch 2, CL)—corner made; sk next 3 sc, in next sc work (CL, ch 1, CL); rep from † to † 49 times more; sk next 2 sc, in next sc work (CL, ch 2, CL, ch 2, CL)—corner made; rep from †† to †† 3 times; join in first dc.

Finish off and weave in all ends.

Assembly

Hold one blue panel and one pink panel with wrong sides together, long edges at top and strip center stitches facing in same direction. Carefully matching stitches on both panels, with tapestry needle and white, sew loosely with overcast stitch in BLs only (see Stitch Guide on page 5) across long edge, beginning and ending with second cluster of corner.

Repeat with remaining panels, alternating colors and having first and last panel in blue.

crochet

Kitty Cat Lullaby

Size:
About 35" x 45"

Materials:
Sport weight yarn, 5 oz (475 yds, 150 g) each, blue and pink; 4 oz (380 yds, 120 g) each, yellow, green, and white
Size G aluminum crochet hook, or size required for gauge

Gauge:
4 hdc= 1"
7 hdc rows = 2"
one square = $7\frac{1}{2}$" x $7\frac{1}{2}$"

Pattern Stitch

Popcorn (PC):
5 dc in st indicated; drop lp from hook, insert hook in first dc made, draw dropped lp through—PC made.

Instructions

Square (make 6 each of pink and blue; make 4 each of yellow and green)
Ch 30 loosely.

Row 1 (right side):
Hdc in 3rd ch from hook (beg 2 skipped chs count as an hdc) and in each rem ch. Ch 2 (counts as first hdc on following rows), turn—29 hdc.

Row 2:
Hdc in each hdc and in 2nd ch of beg 2 skipped chs. Ch 2, turn.

Row 3:
Hdc in each hdc and in 2nd ch of turning ch-2. Ch 2, turn.

Row 4:
Rep Row 3.

Row 5:
Hdc in next 8 hdc, [PC (see Pattern Stitch) in next hdc, hdc in next hdc] 6 times; hdc in next 7 hdc and in 2nd ch of turning ch-2. Ch 2, turn.

Row 6:
Hdc in each hdc, in each PC, and in 2nd ch of turning ch-2. Ch 2, turn.

Row 7:
Hdc in next 6 hdc, PC in next hdc; hdc in next 4 hdc, (PC in next hdc, hdc in next hdc) 5 times; hdc in next 6 hdc and in 2nd ch of turning ch-2. Ch 2, turn.

Row 8:
Rep Row 6.

Row 9:
Hdc in next 5 hdc, PC in next hdc; hdc in next 4 hdc, (PC in next hdc, hdc in next hdc) 6 times; hdc in next 5 hdc and in 2nd ch of turning ch-2. Ch 2, turn.

Row 10:
Rep Row 6.

Row 11:
Hdc in next 5 hdc, PC in next hdc; hdc in next 5 hdc, (PC in next hdc, hdc in next hdc) 5 times; hdc in next 6 hdc and in 2nd ch of turning ch-2. Ch 2, turn.

Row 12:
Rep Row 6.

Row 13:
Hdc in next 6 hdc, PC in next hdc; hdc in next 5 hdc, (PC in next hdc, hdc in next hdc) 4 times; hdc in next 7 hdc and in 2nd ch of turning ch-2. Ch 2, turn.

Row 14:
Rep Row 6.

Row 15:
Hdc in next 13 hdc, (PC in next hdc, hdc in next hdc) 3 times; hdc in next 8 hdc and in 2nd ch of turning ch-2. Ch 2, turn.

Row 16:
Rep Row 6.

Row 17:
Hdc in next 12 hdc, (PC in next hdc, hdc in next hdc) 4 times; hdc in next 7 hdc and in 2nd ch of turning ch-2. Ch 2, turn.

Row 18:
Rep Row 6.

Row 19:
Hdc in next 13 hdc, (PC in next hdc, hdc in next hdc) 3 times; hdc in next 8 hdc and in 2nd ch of turning ch-2. Ch 2, turn.

Row 20:
Rep Row 6.

continued on page 46

Row 21:
Hdc in next 12 hdc, PC in next hdc; hdc in next 5 hdc, PC in next hdc; hdc in next 8 hdc and in 2nd ch of turning ch-2. Ch 2, turn.

Row 22:
Rep Row 6.

Rows 23 through 25:
Rep Row 3. At end of Row 25, ch 1; do not turn.

Trim:
Rnd 1:
Working along side in sps formed by edge hdc and turning chs, sc in Rows 25 through 1; working in unused lps of beg ch, 3 sc in next lp—corner made; sc in next 27 lps, 3 sc in next lp—corner made; working along side in sps formed by edge hdc and turning ch, sc in Rows 1 through 25; working across Row 25, 3 sc in 2nd ch of turning ch—corner made; sc in next 27 hdc, 3 sc in next hdc—corner made; join in first sc—116 sc. Change to white by drawing lp through; cut working color.

Rnd 2:
Ch 1, sc in same sc and in next 25 sc; 3 sc in next sc—corner made; sc in next 29 sc, 3 sc in next sc—corner made; sc in next 27 sc, 3 sc in next sc—corner made; sc in next 29 sc, 3 sc in next sc—corner made; sc in next sc; join in first sc.

Finish off and weave in ends.

Assembly

Referring to **Diagram A** for color and placement of squares, begin at lower left corner of afghan with Square A. Join Square B to Square A. Work remainder of Row 1; then continue with Rows 2 through 5.

Row 5	C Pink	D Blue	D Pink	E Blue
Row 4	C Green	D Yellow	D Green	E Yellow
Row 3	C Pink	D Blue	D Pink	E Blue
Row 2	C Green	D Yellow	D Green	E Yellow
Row 1	A Pink	B Blue	B Pink	B Blue

Diagram A

Square A
Hold square with right side facing you and Row 25 at top; with white, make lp on hook and join with an sc in first sc of 3-sc corner in upper right-hand corner of square; ch 3, sk next sc; * sc in next sc, ch 3, sk next sc; rep from * around; join in joining sc—62 ch-3 sps. Finish off.

Square B
Hold square with right side facing you and Row 25 at top; with white, make lp on hook and join with an sc in first sc of 3-sc corner in upper right-hand corner of square; ch 3, sk next sc; † sc in next sc, ch 3, sk next sc †; rep from † to † 14 times more; sc in next sc, ch 2; hold completed square with wrong side facing wrong side of working square (see **Diagram A**) and with stitches in the same direction and corresponding rows matching; on completed square, sl st in corresponding corner ch-3 sp, ch 2; on working square, sk next sc, sc in next sc; †† ch 1; on completed square, sl st in next ch-3 sp, ch 1; on working square, sk next sc, sc in next sc ††; rep from †† to †† 13 times more; ch 2; on completed square, sl st in next ch-3 sp, ch 2; on working square, sk next sc; rep from † to † 30 times; join in joining sc. Finish off.

Square C
Hold square with right side facing you and Row 25 at top; with white, make lp on hook and join with an sc in first sc of 3-sc corner in upper right-hand corner of square; ch 3, sk next sc; † sc in next sc, ch 3, sk next sc †; rep from † to † 29 times more; sc in next sc, ch 2; hold completed square with wrong side facing wrong side of working square (see **Diagram A**) and with stitches in same direction and corresponding rows matching; on completed square, sl st in corresponding corner ch-3 sp, ch 2; on working square, sk next sc, sc in next sc; †† ch 1; on completed square, sl st in next ch-3 sp, ch 1; on working square, sk next sc, sc in next sc ††; rep from †† to †† 14 times more; ch 2; on completed square, sl st in joining of prev joined squares; ch 2; on working square, sk next sc; rep from † to † 14 times; join in joining sc. Finish off.

Square D
Hold square with right side facing you and Row 25 at top; with white, make lp on hook and join with an sc in first sc of 3-sc corner in upper right-hand corner of square; ch 3, sk next sc; † sc in next sc, ch 3, sk next sc †; rep from † to † 14 times more; sc in next sc, ch 2; hold completed square with wrong side facing wrong side of working square (see **Diagram A**) and with stitches in same direction and corresponding rows matching; on completed square, sl st in corresponding corner ch-3 sp, ch 2; on working square, sk next sc, sc in next sc; †† ch 1; on completed square, sl st in next ch-3 sp, ch 1;

on working square, sk next sc, sc in next sc ††; rep from †† to †† 13 times more; ch 2; on completed square, sl st in center of sl st joining of prev joined squares, ch 2; on working square, sk next sc, sc in next sc; rep from †† to †† 15 times; ch 2; on completed square, sl st in joining of prev joined squares, ch 2; on working square, sk next sc; rep from † to † 14 times; join in joining sc. Finish off.

Square E

Hold square with right side facing you and Row 25 at top; with white, make lp on hook and join with an sc in first sc of 3-sc corner in upper right-hand corner of square; ch 3, sk next sc; † sc in next sc, ch 3, sk next sc †; rep from † to † 14 times more; sc in next sc, ch 2; hold completed square with wrong side facing wrong side of working square (see **Diagram A**) and with stitches in same direction and corresponding rows matching; on completed square, sl st in corresponding corner ch-3 sp, ch 2; on working square, sk next sc, sc in next sc; †† ch 1; on completed square, sl st in next ch-3 sp, ch 1; on working square, sk next sc, sc in next sc ††; rep from †† to †† 13 times more; ch 2; on completed square, sl st in joining of prev joined squares, ch 2; on working square, sk next sc, sc in next sc; rep from †† to †† 15 times; ch 2; on completed square, sl st in corresponding corner ch-3 sp; ch 2; on working square, sk next sc; rep from † to † 14 times; join in joining sc. Finish off.

Border

Hold afghan with right side facing you and Row 5 at top; with white, make lp on hook and join with an sc in ch-3 sp in upper right-hand corner; ch 3; * sc in next sp, ch 3; rep from * around; join in joining sc.

Finish off and weave in all ends.

Lavender and Lace

Size:
About 33" x 39"

Materials:
Baby weight yarn, 10 oz (1700 yds, 300 g) lavender; 3 oz (510 yds, 90 g) white
Size D aluminum crochet hook, or size required for gauge

Gauge:
6 sc = 1"

Instructions

Ch 263 loosely.

Center

Row 1 (wrong side)**:**
Sc in 2nd ch from hook; * sk next 3 chs, in each of next 2 chs work (dc, ch 2, dc); sk next 3 chs, sc in next ch; rep from * 28 times more. Ch 1, turn.

Row 2 (right side)**:**
Sc in first sc; * in next ch-2 sp work (hdc, 3 dc); in next ch-2 sp work (3 dc, hdc); sc in next sc; rep from * across. Ch 7 (counts as first trc and ch-3 sp on following rows), turn.

Row 3:
Sk next 3 sts, sc in next 2 dc; * ch 7, sk next 7 sts, sc in next 2 dc; rep from * across to last 4 sts; ch 3, sk next 3 sts, trc in last sc. Ch 1, turn.

Row 4:
Sc in first trc, in each of next 2 sc work (dc, ch 2, dc); * sc in next ch-7 sp, in each of next 2 sc work (dc, ch 2, dc); rep from * to turning ch-7; sk next 3 chs of turning ch-7, sc in next ch. Ch 1, turn.

Rows 5 through 148:
Rep Rows 2 through 4 forty-eight times more.

Rows 149 and 150:
Rep Rows 2 and 3. At end of Row 150, do not ch 1; do not turn.

Finish off and weave in all ends.

Border

Hold center with right side facing you and Row 150 at top; join white in ch-3 sp in upper right-hand corner.

Rnd 1:
Ch 1, 6 sc in same sp; * sc in next 2 sc, 6 sc in next ch-7 sp; rep from * 27 times more; sc in next 2 sc, 10 sc in sp formed by turning ch-7; working across next side in edge sc and in sps formed by turning chs, † (sc in next 2 edge sc, 4 sc in next sp) 49 times †; sc in next 2 edge sc, 8 sc in next sp; working in unused lps and skipped chs of beg ch, sc in next 2 lps, (3 sc in each of next 2 ch-3 sps, sc in next 2 lps) 28 times; 8 sc in next lp; working along next side in edge sc and in sps formed by turning chs; rep from † to † once; sc in next 2 edge sc, 4 sc in side of next trc; join in first sc—1080 sc.

Rnd 2:
Ch 1, sc in same sc; † (ch 3, sl st in 3rd ch from hook—picot made) 3 times †; sc in next sc; * ch 5, sk next 4 sc, sc in next sc; rep from † to † once; sc in next sc; rep from * to last 4 sc; ch 2, sk last 4 sc; join with a dc in first sc.

Rnd 3:
Ch 1, sc in sp formed by joining dc; ch 10; * sc in next ch-5 sp, ch 10; rep from * around; join in first sc.

Rnd 4:
Ch 1, sc in same sc; 13 sc in next ch-10 sp; * sc in next sc, 13 sc in next ch-10 sp; rep from * around; join in first sc.

Rnd 5:
Sl st in BLs only of next 2 sc, picot; * (sk next sc, sl st in BL of next sc, picot) 5 times; sk next 3 sc, sl st in BL of next sc, picot; rep from * around; join in first sl st. Finish off.

Rnd 6:
Join white in first picot; ch 3, (sl st in next picot, ch 3) 4 times; sk next picot; * (sl st in next picot, ch 3) 5 times; sk next picot; rep from * around; join in first ch of beg ch-3.

Finish off and weave in ends.

crochet

Little Angel

Size:
About 33" x 42"

Materials:
Baby weight yarn, 13½ oz (2295 yds, 405 g) white
Size D aluminum crochet hook, or size required for gauge

Gauge:
6 sc = 1"
motif = 2½" x 2½"

Instructions

Note: Motif patterns follow assembly instructions.

Assembly

Beg at lower left of afghan, work Motif A. Work Motif B, joining to Motif A in last rnd. Referring to **Diagram A** for placement of motifs, work remainder of afghan.

Diagram A

Motif Patterns

Motif A:
Ch 4, join to form a ring.

Rnd 1 (right side)**:**
Ch 1, 8 sc in ring; join in first sc.

Rnd 2:
Ch 1, 2 sc in same sc and in each rem sc; join in first sc—16 sc.

Rnd 3:
Ch 3 **(**counts as an hdc and a ch-1 sp**)**, **(**hdc in next sc, ch 1**)** 15 times; join in 2nd ch of beg ch-3—16 hdc.

Rnd 4:
Ch 1, sc in same ch as joining, in each ch-1 sp, and in each hdc; join in first sc—32 sc.

Rnd 5:
Ch 4 **(**counts as an hdc and a ch-2 sp**)**, sk next sc, hdc in next sc, **(**ch 2, sk next sc, hdc in next sc**)** 14 times; ch 2; join in 2nd ch of beg ch-4.

Rnd 6:
Ch 1, sc in same ch as joining; ***** † ch 3, sk next ch-2 sp, in next ch-2 sp work **(**3 dc, ch 3, 3 dc**)**—corner made; ch 3, sk next ch-2 sp, sc in next hdc, ch 3 †; sk next ch-2 sp, sc in next hdc; rep from ***** twice more, then rep from † to † once; join in first sc.

Finish off and weave in ends.

Motif B:
Work same as Motif A through Rnd 5.

Rnd 6:
Ch 1, sc in same ch as joining; ***** ch 3, sk next ch-2 sp, in next ch-2 sp work **(**3 dc, ch 3, 3 dc**)**—corner made; **(**ch 3, sk next ch-2 sp, sc in next hdc**)** twice; rep from ***** twice more; ch 3, sk next ch-2 sp, 3 dc in next ch-2 sp; ch 1, sl st in ch-3 sp of any corner of first motif, ch 1; 3 dc in same sp on working motif—joined corner made; ch 3, sk next ch-2 sp, sc in next hdc, ch 3; join in first sc.

Finish off and weave in ends.

Motif C:
Work same as Motif A through Rnd 5.

Rnd 6:
Ch 1, sc in same ch as joining; ***** ch 3, sk next ch-2 sp, in next ch-2 sp work **(**3 dc, ch 3, 3 dc**)**—corner made; **(**ch 3, sk next ch-2 sp, sc in next hdc**)** twice; rep from ***** twice

continued on page 52

more; ch 3, sk next ch-2 sp, 3 dc in next ch-2 sp; ch 1, sl st in corner ch-3 sp of prev motif opposite joined corner (see **Diagram A** on page 50); ch 1; 3 dc in same sp on working motif—joined corner made; ch 3, sk next ch-2 sp, sc in next hdc, ch 3; join in first sc.

Finish off and weave in ends.

Motif D:
Work same as Motif A through Rnd 5.

Rnd 6:
Ch 1, sc in same ch as joining; ch 3, sk next ch-2 sp, in next ch-2 sp work (3 dc, ch 3, 3 dc)—corner made; (ch 3, sk next ch-2 sp, sc in next hdc) twice; ch 3, sk next ch-2 sp, 3 dc in next ch-2 sp; ch 1, sl st in corner ch-3 sp at top of motif [see (a) on **Diagram A** on page 50]; ch 1, 3 dc in same sp on working motif; † ch 1, sl st in next ch-3 sp on completed motif; ch 1, sk next ch-2 sp on working motif, sc in next hdc †; rep from † to † once more; ch 1, sl st in next ch-3 sp on completed motif; ch 1, sk next ch-2 sp on working motif, 3 dc in next ch-2 sp; ch 1, sl st in joining of motifs, ch 1, 3 dc in same sp on working motif; rep from † to † twice; ch 1, sl st in next ch-3 sp on completed motif; ch 1, sk next ch-2 sp on working motif, 3 dc in next ch-2 sp; ch 1, sl st in corner ch-3 sp on completed motif; ch 1, 3 dc in same sp on working motif; ch 3, sk next ch-2 sp, sc in next hdc, ch 3; join in first sc.

Finish off and weave in ends.

Motif E:
Work same as Motif A through Rnd 5.

Rnd 6:
Ch 1, sc in same ch as joining; ch 3, sk next ch-2 sp, in next ch-2 sp work (3 dc, ch 3, 3 dc)—corner made; (ch 3, sk next ch-2 sp, sc in next hdc) twice; ch 3, sk next ch-2 sp, 3 dc in next ch-2 sp; ch 1, sl st in joining of motifs [see (b) on **Diagram A** on page 50]; ch 1, 3 dc in same sp on working motif; † ch 1, sl st in next ch-3 sp on completed motif; ch 1, sk next ch-2 sp on working motif, sc in next hdc †; rep from † to † once more; ch 1, sl st in next ch-3 sp on completed motif; ch 1, sk next ch-2 sp on working motif, 3 dc in next ch-2 sp; ch 1, sl st in joining of motifs; ch 1, 3 dc in same sp on working motif; rep from † to † twice; ch 1, sl st in next ch-3 sp on completed motif; ch 1, sk next ch-2 sp on working motif, 3 dc in next ch-2 sp; ch 1, sl st in corner ch-3 sp on completed motif; ch 1, 3 dc in same sp on working motif; ch 3, sk next ch-2 sp, sc in next hdc, ch 3; join in first sc.

Finish off and weave in ends.

Motif F:
Work same as Motif A through Rnd 5.

Rnd 6:
Ch 1, sc in same ch as joining; ch 3, sk next ch-2 sp, in next ch-2 sp work (3 dc, ch 3, 3 dc)—corner made; (ch 3, sk next ch-2 sp, sc in next hdc) twice; ch 3, sk next ch-2 sp, in next ch-2 sp work (3 dc, ch 3, 3 dc)—corner made; (ch 3, sk next ch-2 sp, sc in next hdc) twice; ch 3, sk next ch-2 sp, 3 dc in next ch-2 sp; ch 1, sl st in joining of motifs [see (a) on **Diagram A** on page 50]; ch 1, 3 dc in same sp on working motif; † ch 1, sl st in next ch-3 sp on completed motif; ch 1, sk next ch-2 sp on working motif, sc in next hdc †; rep from † to † once more; ch 1, sl st in next ch-3 sp on completed motif; ch 1, 3 dc in next ch-2 sp on working motif; ch 1, sl st in corner ch-3 sp on completed motif; ch 1, 3 dc in same sp on working motif; ch 3, sk next ch-2 sp, sc in next hdc, ch 3; join in first sc.

Finish off and weave in ends.

Motif G:
Work same as Motif A through Rnd 5.

Rnd 6:
Ch 1, sc in same ch as joining; ch 3, sk next ch-2 sp, in next ch-2 sp work (3 dc, ch 3, 3 dc)—corner made; (ch 3, sk next ch-2 sp, sc in next hdc) twice; ch 3, sk next ch-2 sp, 3 dc in next ch-2 sp; ch 1, sl st in joining of motifs [see (c) on **Diagram A** on page 50]; ch 1, 3 dc in same sp on working motif; † ch 1, sl st in next ch-3 sp on completed motif; ch 1, sk next ch-2 sp on working motif, sc in next hdc †; rep from † to † once more; ch 1, sl st in next ch-3 sp on completed motif; ch 1, sk next ch-2 sp on working motif, 3 dc in next ch-2 sp; ch 1, sl st in next joining of motifs; ch 1, 3 dc in same sp on working motif; rep from † to † twice; ch 1, sl st in next ch-3 sp on completed motif; ch 1, sk next ch-2 sp on working motif, 3 dc in next ch-2 sp; ch 1, sl st in corner ch-3 sp on completed motif; ch 1, 3 dc in same sp on working motif; ch 3, sk next ch-2 sp, sc in next hdc, ch 3; join in first sc.

Finish off and weave in ends.

Motif H:
Work same as Motif A through Rnd 5.

Rnd 6:
Ch 1, sc in same ch as joining; ch 3, sk next ch-2 sp, in next ch-2 sp work (3 dc, ch 3, 3 dc)—corner made; (ch 3, sk next ch-2 sp, sc in next hdc) twice; ch 3, sk next ch-2 sp, 3 dc in next ch-2 sp; ch 1, sl st in joining of motifs [see (d) on **Diagram A** on page 50]; ch 1, 3 dc in same sp on working motif; † ch 1, sl st in next ch-3 sp on

completed motif; ch 1, sk next ch-2 sp on working motif, sc in next hdc †; rep from † to † once more; ch 1, sl st in next ch-3 sp on completed motif; ch 1, 3 dc in next ch-2 sp on working motif; ch 1, sl st in next joining of motifs; ch 1, 3 dc in same sp on working motif; (ch 3, sk next ch-2 sp, sc in next hdc) twice; ch 3, sk next ch-2 sp, in next ch-2 sp work (3 dc, ch 3, 3 dc)—corner made; ch 3, sk next ch-2 sp, sc in next hdc, ch 3; join in first sc.

Finish off and weave in ends.

Edging

Hold afghan with right side facing you and one short end at top; join yarn in first unused corner ch-3 sp of motif in upper right-hand corner [see (e) on **Diagram A** on page 50].

Rnd 1:
Ch 1, sc in same sp; † (ch 5, sc in next ch-3 sp) 7 times; ch 5, sc in joining of motifs †; rep from † to † 8 times more; (ch 5, sc in next ch-3 sp) 11 times; ch 5, sc in joining of motifs; rep from † to † 11 times; (ch 5, sc in next ch-3 sp) 11 times; ch 5, sc in joining of motifs; rep from † to † 8 times; (ch 5, sc in next ch-3 sp) 11 times; ch 5, sc in joining of motifs; rep from † to † 11 times; (ch 5, sc in next ch-3 sp) 3 times; ch 5; join in first sc.

Rnd 2:
Sl st in next ch-5 sp, in same sp work (3 sc, ch 3, sl st in last sc made—picot made; 2 sc); in each of next 6 ch-5 sps work (3 sc, ch 3, sl st in last sc—picot made; 2 sc); 3 sc in each of next 2 ch-5 sps; † in each of next 6 sps work (3 sc, picot, 2 sc); 3 sc in each of next 2 ch-5 sps †; rep from † to † 7 times more; in each of next 10 ch-3 sps work (3 sc, picot, 2 sc); 3 sc in each of next 2 ch-5 sps; rep from † to † 11 times; in each of next 10 ch-5 sps work (3 sc, picot, 2 sc); 3 sc in each of next 2 ch-5 sps; rep from † to † 11 times; in each of next 3 ch-5 sps work (3 sc, picot, 2 sc); join in first sc.

Finish off and weave in all ends.

Little Fisherman

Size:
About 35" x 42" before fringe

Materials:
Sport weight yarn, 20 oz (1900 yds, 600 g) ecru
Size 6, 36" circular knitting needle, or size required for gauge
Cable needle

Gauge:
5 sts = 1" in stockinette stitch (knit one row, purl one row)

Pattern Stitches

Back Twist (BT):
Sl next 2 sts onto cable needle and hold in back of work; knit next st, knit 2 sts from cable needle—BT made.

Front Twist (FT):
Sl next st onto cable needle and hold in front of work; knit next 2 sts, knit st from cable needle—FT made.

Instructions

Cast on 232 sts.

Row 1 (right side):
* K 1, P1; rep from * across.

Row 2:
* P1, K1; rep from * across.

Rows 3 through 6:
Rep Rows 1 and 2 twice more.

Row 7:
(K1, P1) twice; K1; * P3, (yb, sl 1 as to knit, K2, PSSO two sts, P2) twice; P1, K12; rep from * 7 times more; P3, (yb, sl 1 as to knit, K2, PSSO two sts, P2) twice; P1, (P1, K1) twice; P1.

Row 8:
(P1, K1) twice; P1; * K3, (P1, YO, P1, K2) twice; K1, (P4, sl next 2 sts as to purl) twice; rep from * 7 times more; K3, (P1, YO, P1, K2) twice; K1, (K1, P1) twice; K1.

Row 9:
(K1, P1) twice; K1; * P3, (K3, P2) twice; P1, [BT (see Pattern Stitches), FT (see Pattern Stitches) twice; rep from * 7 times more; P3, (K3, P2) twice; P1, (P1, K1) twice; P1.

Row 10:
(P1, K1) twice; P1; * K3, (P3, K2) twice; K1, P12; rep from * 7 times more; K3, (P3, K2) twice; K1, (K1, P1) twice; K1.

Row 11:
Rep Row 7.

Row 12:
(P1, K1) twice; P1; * K3, (P1, YO, P1, K2) twice; K1, yf, sl 1 as to purl, P4, sl next 2 sts as to purl, P4, sl 1 as to purl; rep from * 7 times more; K3, (P1, YO, P1, K2) twice; K1, (K1, P1) twice; K1.

Row 13:
(K1, P1) twice; K1; * P3, (K3, P2) twice; P1, (FT, BT) twice; rep from * 7 times more; P3, (K3, P2) twice; P1, (P1, K1) twice; P1.

Row 14:
Rep Row 10.

Rows 15 through 318:
Rep Rows 7 through 14 thirty-eight times more.

Rows 319 through 324:
Rep Rows 1 through 6.

Bind off in pattern.

Fringe

Following Fringe Instructions on page 6, make Triple Knot Fringe. Cut 27" strands; use 8 strands for each knot. Tie knots evenly spaced across cast on edge only of afghan, to avoid having fringe close to baby's face.

Lullaby and Goodnight

Size:
About 33" x 42"

Materials:
Baby weight yarn, 12 oz (2040 yds, 360 g) mint
Size D aluminum crochet hook, or size required for gauge

Gauge:
6 dc = 1"
3 dc rows = 1"

Instructions

Ch 217 loosely.

Center

Row 1 (right side)**:**
3 dc in 4th ch from hook (beg 3 skipped chs count as a dc); sk next 4 chs, 4 dc in next ch; * ch 3, sk next 3 chs, sc in next ch, ch 3, sk next 3 chs, 4 dc in next ch; sk next 4 chs, 4 dc in next ch; rep from * 15 times more. Ch 3 (counts as first dc on following rows), turn.

Row 2:
3 dc in first dc; sk next 6 dc; * 4 dc in next dc; ch 3, sc in next sc, ch 3, 4 dc in next dc; sk next 6 dc; rep from * 15 times more; 4 dc in 3rd ch of beg 3 skipped chs. Ch 6 (counts as first dc and ch-3 sp on following rows), turn.

Row 3:
Sc between first two 4-dc groups, ch 3; * sk next 3 dc, 4 dc in next dc; sk next sc, 4 dc in next dc; ch 3, sc between same 4-dc group and next 4-dc group, ch 3; rep from * 15 times more; sk next 3 dc, dc in 3rd ch of turning ch-3. Ch 6, turn.

Row 4:
Sc in next sc, ch 3; * 4 dc in next dc; sk next 6 dc, 4 dc in next dc; ch 3, sc in next sc, ch 3; rep from * 15 times more; sk next 3 chs of turning ch-6, dc in next ch. Ch 3, turn.

Row 5:
3 dc in first dc; * sk next sc, 4 dc in next dc; ch 3, sc between same 4-dc group and next 4-dc group, ch 3, sk next 3 dc, 4 dc in next dc; rep from * 15 times more; sk next sc and next 3 chs of turning ch-6; 4 dc in next ch of turning ch. Ch 3, turn.

Row 6:
3 dc in first dc; sk next 6 dc; * 4 dc in next dc; ch 3, sc in next sc, ch 3, 4 dc in next dc; sk next 6 dc; rep from * 15 times more; 4 dc in 3rd ch of turning ch-3. Ch 6, turn.

Rows 7 through 110:
Rep Rows 3 through 6 twenty-four times more. At end of Row 110, do not ch 6. Ch 1, turn.

Border

Rnd 1:
Ch 1, sc in first 8 dc; * 2 sc in each of next 2 ch-3 sps; sc in next 8 dc; rep from * 14 times more; 2 sc in each of next 2 ch-3 sps; sc in next 7 dc and in 3rd ch of turning ch-3; working along next side in ends of rows, 2 sc in each row; working along next side in unused lps of beg chs and in sps formed by skipped chs, sc in first unused lp; ** 3 sc in next sp; sc in next unused lp; rep from ** 48 times more; working along next side in ends of rows, 2 sc in each row; join in first sc—837 sc.

Rnd 2:
Ch 1, sc in same sc; sk next 2 sc, 5 dc in next sc; sk next 2 sc, sc in next sc, ch 2, sk next 2 sc; * sc in next sc, sk next 2 sc, 5 dc in next sc; sk next 2 sc, sc in next sc, ch 2, sk next 2 sc; rep from * around; join in first sc.

Rnd 3:
Sl st in next dc, ch 4 (counts as a dc and a ch-1 sp), (dc in next dc, ch 1) 3 times; dc in next dc, sc in next ch-2 sp; * (dc in next dc, ch 1) 4 times; dc in next dc, sc in next ch-2 sp; rep from * around; join in 3rd ch of beg ch-4.

Rnd 4:
Ch 5 (counts as a dc and a ch-2 sp), (dc in next dc, ch 2) 3 times; * keeping last lp of each dc on hook, dc in next dc, sk next sc, dc in next sc, YO and draw through all 3 lps on hook; ch 2, (dc in next dc, ch 2) 3 times; rep from * to last dc; dc in last dc; join in 3rd ch of beg ch-5.

Rnd 5:
* † Ch 3, 7 dc in next ch-2 sp; drop lp from hook, insert hook in first dc, draw dropped lp through—PC made †; ch 3, sl st in next st; rep from * to last ch-2 sp; rep from † to † once; join in joining sl st. Finish off.

Rnd 6:
Join yarn in FL of 4th dc of last PC made; ch 1, draw up lp in same sp, draw up lp in FL of 4th dc of next PC, YO and draw through all 3 lps on hook; ch 7, (sl st in FL of 4th dc of next PC, ch 7) twice; * draw up lp in FL of 4th dc of each of next 2 PCs, YO and draw through all 3 lps on hook; ch 7, (sl st in FL of 4th dc of next PC, ch 7) twice; rep from * around; join in first st.

Rnd 7:
* Ch 7, sl st in next st; rep from * around; join in joining sl st.

Finish off and weave in all ends.